One man's story of
coming to terms with
autism and ADHD

STAIRWAY

TO THE

SPECTRUM

TRAVIS ALEXANDER

Copyright © 2025 Travis Alexander

Travis Alexander asserts the moral right to be identified as the author of this work.

All rights reserved. No part of this publication may be reproduced, stored in a retrieval system, or transmitted, in any form or by any means electronic, mechanical, photocopying, recording or otherwise, without the prior permission of the author.

This memoir is an honest account of my life living with undiagnosed autism, ADHD and dyslexia into adulthood. The story encompasses real-life experiences and my personal struggles from being held captive by the conditions with little to no support. With the exception of myself as the main character, names and locations have been changed to protect privacy, and I have done my very best to achieve this without sacrificing the truth of the story.

Book cover design and formatting by Author Services Australia.

eBook ISBN: 978-1-7638054-0-8
Paperback ISBN: 978-1-7638054-1-5
Audiobook ISBN: 978-1-7638054-2-2

For the neurodivergent community.
The world needs us!

CONTENTS

INTRODUCTION vii

ACT 1: HIGH SCHOOL 1
Chapters One to Chapter Twenty-Two

ACT 2: UNIVERSITY AND EARLY-CAREER 101
Chapters Twenty-Three to Chapter Forty-Four

ACT 3: ADULT LIFE WITH DIAGNOSIS 221
Chapters Forty-Five to Fifty

INTRODUCTION

ACCORDING TO RESEARCH at the time of writing, 1 in 10 people in Australia are dyslexic, 1 in 20 people have an attention deficit hyperactivity disorder (ADHD) and 1 in 40 have an autism spectrum disorder (ASD).[4] That's 2.7 million, 1.35 million and 675,000 neurodivergent Australians respectively. But what's more alarming is that more than half don't receive an official diagnosis and therefore don't manage it, which prevents them reaching their full potential.[1] This is not only a terrifying experience for high school students, but also a serious problem for adults. Without proper guidance, life can take a wrong turn and easily spiral out of control. In Australia, if you're autistic you're half as likely to complete year 10 and three times more likely to be unemployed than someone with another disability.[3] I'm not surprised we're at higher risk of hanging out with the wrong crowds, alcohol and drug abuse, incarceration, and divorce as well as depression, suicide, eating and anxiety disorders.

I strongly believe that sharing our stories of what it's really like living day-to-day with these conditions is crucial for understanding and survival. I know there are many people out there who are completely unaware of carrying one or more of these conditions. I hope this story finds its way into the youth so they can understand the importance of self-awareness, and work on building themselves a very possible bright future. Improved self-awareness paves the way for better decision-making, communication and relationships along with a real potential to achieve success and make a big impact on the world. Famous neurodivergent individuals such as Albert Einstein, Bill Gates, Greta Thunberg and Elon Musk have done it before, and it can certainly be done again.

In my story, I want to entertain, enlighten, educate, and fuel positive emotions in the neurodivergent population to live their best lives. I also aim to provide an insight into what goes on inside our heads, because research shows that 84% of people in Australia know the word autism but only 29% have a knowledge of what it actually means.[3]

At the time of writing, neurodiversity has only recently become a hot topic. Autism is currently under the national spotlight: the Australian government has just appointed its first ever minister for autism, to help craft its first national autism strategy.[3] This, along with current reform of the National Disability Insurance Scheme (NDIS), is paving the way for better treatment of the neurodivergent population and supporting their enormous strengths and high value added to the world.

ACT 1
HIGH SCHOOL

CHAPTER ONE

HAVE YOU EVER wanted to get revenge on a bully? Someone intimidating, with more social power who enjoys making your life a nightmare. Someone who is spoken poorly about but rarely (if ever) gets a taste of their own medicine. When I was young, I couldn't help myself.

"Are they open?" I said, pointing at the hardware store.

Peter abruptly stopped talking.

Like a nutty professor I always had lots of crazy ideas but seldom shared them with friends. They were random and too spontaneous for anyone to take seriously.

When I told him what I wanted to buy he jumped. When I told him why his tanned cheeks turned red before his body tensed, like it was about to brace itself before a tackle.

"Travis! I can't be seen in there with you." Peter said.

His response didn't faze me. Peter's image means everything to him. One time we missed the bus after my dad and I waited outside his house an extra seven minutes, while he was in the bathroom spoofing his greasy hair with gel.

"Bloody wogs," dad would say jokingly.

I waited until he was out of sight before heading in. Hearing the creaking floorboards and taking in the scent of hay, it wasn't long before being approached by the owner.

"Morning mate, what are you after?"

"Bolt cutters," I replied.

He gave me a strange look then scratched his head like I'd given him a hard task.

"Down the hall, to the left," he said.

For a small shopfront selling farm animal products, I was surprised to see so many different sizes. I grabbed the largest set which would fit inside my backpack, then headed for the counter.

He squinted.

"What do you want these for?" the owner said.

My body froze as his question caught me off guard.

I stuttered, "I can't get into ma ma my locker,"

"Doesn't your school have a set?" he replied.

I remember pinching my fingernails on my sleeves thinking he recognised me. Flat Rock was only a small town and many people knew my dad, the jolly man who always said g'day. We lived there my whole life. When I was eight my family moved houses and even though it was only a kilometre away, I struggled to adjust with the change.

I hesitantly shook my head.

The owner rolled his eyes while I tried to act cool, waiting for the EFTPOS machine to accept my $46.50. Luckily, he didn't ask any more questions.

By the time I arrived at the bus my back was aching from the heavy blade digging into my back.

"Hurry up!" The driver yelled over the engine.

I sat down in the vacant seat in front of Peter as we took off. He whispered. "Did you get them?"

I nodded. Then turning around I un-zipped a section of the bag. He arched forward lifting his chin over the backrest before his mouth dropped open.

The expression of horror on his face should've signalled to me what I was about to do was very wrong, but at the time I was oblivious of the fire burning inside me. If only I was more aware of my own emotions.

Peter Coobey was the new kid in Flat Rock looking to make a good impression. Three years earlier his family moved into a house around the corner from us. They'd moved down from Brisbane after his dad was promoted to a higher management role.

I remember meeting him for the first time when walking past his house. Peter was out in the front yard polishing his dad's convertible. The family owned two brand new BMWs and upgraded to the newer model every few years.

Mesmerized by the car I yelled out, "Nice wheels mate!" They were the only two words needed for Peter to hold me up another forty minutes. I couldn't shut him up that day. We've been close friends ever since.

My whole body shifted forward as the bus's brakes brought everything to a halt. Out the window I could see his red hair gleaming in the sunlight. I swallowed hard making sure my bag was tucked away. The bus had pulled up at the next stop and I knew he would sit next to me. My eyes made contact with his shoes walking down the aisle before looking away, pretending to focus on something else.

Within seconds I felt the brush of wind pass my face and heard a bum landing on the seat.

"Travy! Where's your girlfriend Travy, hey, hey, hey Travy."

With my eyes half closed and face cringed for what I knew was coming, Scott reached for my nipples. Lifting my elbows blocking his skinny arms, he detoured, poking different areas around my abdomen.

"Don't," I said, resisting.

After a few seconds of squeezing, he stopped and stared at me with a satisfying look. As his pointy nose came creeping closer, I leaned back keeping my legs tucked tightly over the bag.

"You'll never get a girlfriend," he said.

Then he turned to face Peter. "You too!"

Peter retaliated by imitating his voice. "Oh, I'm more popular than everyone else!"

I laughed under my breath. He sounded like an Aussie bogan trying to force a British accent. If only it had more impact on his behavior.

CHAPTER TWO

SCOTT READ. I remember when he started dating his girlfriend, he greeted me with the same phrase. It was like the romance had suddenly given him an enormous boost of self-confidence, lifting his social status at school and thereby gaining privileges of dishing out verbal abuse to anyone he pleased.

At the beginning I didn't care so much but as time went on, I would hear the taunts more often. From the corner of my eye, I would see him leave conversations and come over to me with the intention of pointing it out. Most of the time I never responded and tried to ignore it but for some reason, my way of not reacting appeared to give him further indulgence.

Back then I never understood why this was the case and why any girl would be interested in dating someone who belittles others. I was under the impression this is what guys needed to do to get girlfriends and lose their virginity. Fortunately for most of us now in adulthood that's not the case.

Scott's constant reminders left me angry, confused and somewhat jealous. I certainly didn't have a girlfriend during high school, nor did I ever want one. I remember being terrified of talking to girls and would choose my friends based on that principle. There were times I would intentionally detour and sometimes run to avoid any social interaction. I would even pretend to forget girls' names in the hope they'd quickly lose interest. My mates found it hilarious.

When I was in year 11 a girl searching for a debutante ball partner asked me if I wanted to join her.

I immediately shook my head. "I don't do debs, please ask someone else," I replied.

The history of Scott and I goes back to primary school. Living in the same neighborhood, our families knew one another. Growing up we played Rugby, Cricket and Tennis both on the same and opposing teams. I recall playing a Tennis match against Scott in a local competition one night which I happened to lose in a tie-breaker, due to a few unforced errors near the end. Even at the best of times I can't stand losing. A few months earlier I ran off the court prematurely and headed for home because I couldn't handle the shame of losing to a girl.

Scott saw my pain towards losing and would relish the opportunity. The following week after our match he called out to my mum at the Cricket nets. "I beat Trav on Friday night, he isn't a very good tennis player, is he?"

Our mothers sat next to each other on the morning train heading to work, but mum would often move to different locations trying to avoid her. I'd hear stories of Scott's mum sharing how talented her son was,

"He's a bit of a maths whiz," she said.

My mum rolled her eyes as she repeatedly spoke of Scott's scholarship application at South Darlinghurst Grammar. It was the best private boys' school in Sydney. But a few weeks later when my mum questioned for an update she'd reply, "Well, they've invited him to apply again next year."

I remember not long after he was caught cheating on a maths test at school. I had overheard him bragging to someone that he'd got his hands on the answer sheet before offering to sell it to other students. Luckily his teacher was the father of one of our family friends, so I put on my whistleblowing shoes, making sure he didn't get away with it.

Whether because he was the only other ginger in the year or my high level of competitiveness, I had felt an unspoken rivalry, which I always tried to keep to myself. But since achieving his girlfriend status Scott made it more public and confrontational. He was the type of person who had to be one up on you whenever possible.

When we were in year 10, I used to throw apples at the canteen chimney during recess, with the aim of landing it inside. It wasn't long before Scott brought apples to school too. "I got it in, you suck Trav!" he said after his first attempt. For the record it was never confirmed his apple landed in.

In the hope to stop him being annoying and create some separation I turned up at school one day with peroxide blonde hair.

"Look at Trav, he's turned into a parrot," Scott announced to the class.

I remember standing there hot in the face, as Scott egged others on to laugh at me. Then strangely enough, within a month he showed up with peroxide blonde hair too! It was the fad at the time!

Unlike other students, Scott's verbal bashings appeared to affect me on a deeper level. Everyone else could easily brush it aside whereas his words often stayed with me. From a young age my long-term memory has always behaved like a steel-trap. Once something is locked in my head it's virtually impossible to forget it. Over the years I've impressed many people being able to provide dates, events, conversations, and songs with accurate detail. I've accidently freaked people out too. One time I ran into a girl at the dog park knowing her first and last name, the suburb she lived, the school she went to and what she used to do for work. This was ten years after sitting next to her a couple of times in a university lecture.

Her jaw dropped with intense surprise. "I'm sorry, I have no idea who you are," she said.

It's a great skill to have in my toolkit however I've come to realise now some things in life are better off forgotten.

In high school I didn't know how to stand up for myself. Ignoring Scott didn't seem to work and only made me feel worse. If only I had the courage of another boy in our year level who headbutted Scott in the face after he ridiculed his mum. I still remember seeing him walk down the corridors with a black eye.

There was also an element of not knowing how to talk about it, not knowing what to say and who to tell. I had trouble understanding what was going on, why it was happening and what to do to make it stop.

I remember flagging Scott's ongoing verbal abuse twice with year level coordinators but quickly gave up after hearing things like, "We'll keep an eye on it." and "Let us know if it gets worse." I remember thinking they were too busy handling the other troublemakers. Egan High was a government funded school full of no hope students who didn't want to be there.

It's only now I regret not raising the issues with my parents. I didn't like to ask for help and thought involving my parents would only complicate the matter. I also thought deep down I was smarter than him and could handle things myself.

CHAPTER THREE

I HAVE NO complaints about my family or the way I was brought up. I had a loving relationship with my three siblings and parents, who were always supportive of my education and extra-curricular activities. Regularly they drove us on weekends to sporting activities and also offered to help with scoring, umpiring or even getting involved with committee meetings. My dad was president of the local rugby club for three years.

Although great role models I still had challenges growing up. Listening and paying attention has always been and still is one of my greatest evils. Primary school teachers consistently brought it up in their end of year reports with comments like, "easily distracted" and "has trouble following instructions." When I was eight one of them even referred me to see a specialist. I remember an audiologist got me to put on these bulky headphones and measured my responses to different frequencies of sounds. My results were below the threshold for my age, so I was diagnosed with a short-term auditory processing disorder. However when I returned for testing the following year, they said my brain development had caught up and I was no longer below the threshold. As a coping strategy I would often repeat back what a person has said. This would buy myself time to process and understand verbal information. I've come to learn this is called echolalia.

I was also easily obsessed with certain things, for example when dad hung up a map of the world in my bedroom I would come home from school and stare at it for hours, memorizing names of different countries and their capital cities. It impressed the adults, some of which thought I was a little genius. My obsessions changed over time and sometimes became more obscure, for example when I was fourteen I became interested in Osama bin Laden after the 9/11 attacks. Regularly following the news on his whereabouts, I would research up on the names of other members from Al-Qaeda, recite their militant positions, find out their birthdays and practice pronouncing their names in full.

Unless the topic was of high interest I never liked reading because comprehension for me was very hard. Fully grasping the overarching concepts and understanding the information never seemed to stick. During school I got fed up re-reading paragraphs so I often defaulted towards memorization, which played a dominant role in my learning. This technique allowed me to get through but caused a few hiccups along the way.

In year 9 our class sat a test on the definitions of twenty different political terms. I wanted to impress the teacher with the best mark so rather than having my own understanding I memorized textbook definitions word for word as well as the location of commas, capital letters and full stops.

The teacher pressed her lips. "Stay behind please!" she said.

"But I didn't cheat," I replied.

Unfortunately, she still sent me to the principal's office.

Other behavioral challenges most kids grow out of with maturity seemed to linger with me. Sleepwalking and night terrors at one stage were a regular occurrence, both at home and sleepovers. I would wake up in the middle of the night circulating my bedroom under the belief I was trapped inside a cage. Sometimes I'd gasp, sweat and breathe heavy in response to the fear of being chased. When I was nine, I removed the fly screen from my bedroom window, climbed out into the backyard and banged on the door at 3am in the morning! Mum was petrified believing I was a burglar.

Her voice tremored. "Who's there?" she said.

"It's me!" I replied.

Self-inhibition, the ability to stop myself from mischievous behavior was also a problem. Especially when you're influenced by other kids. When I was eleven, I manually turned off all the water troughs in the schoolyard thinking it would be fun to watch everyone go thirsty on a hot day. When I was fourteen, I was with some mates running to catch a train pulling into the station. It was some time before the next one so without even a second thought I took a shortcut, jumping over the fence and landing onto the tracks. With the sound of the horn blaring, I managed to pull myself up onto the platform seconds before being crushed. The driver then left his cockpit to find me hiding inside one of the carriages. I still remember his piercing eyes,

"I hope you're proud of yourself son, you just ruined my day," he said.

Being sent to Egan High didn't seem to help my developmental delays either. The fees were optional which brought in a variety of different students, some of which came from broken home lives. I dreaded going away on school camps because I was forced to spend intimate time with other kids. I remember being pulled aside one time by a teacher asking if I was ok and why I wandered around by myself. I also loathed the times teachers would ask me to read or answer questions in front of the class, even if I knew the correct answer. Oral presentations were also difficult.

You had to choose your friends at school carefully because the bullying and fighting among students was poorly handled and often went undetected. I was bitter with my parents because I wanted to transfer across to the Private school with my best mate Kiel, but they couldn't afford the fees. Mum grew up in a poor family and dad was never smart when it comes to money. Even today in his 60s mum still hands him his weekly allowance so he can head to the liquor store and buy his favourite slab of beer.

I remember having a conversation with a friend about an encounter he had in year 9. A European boy repeatedly called him a deaf cunt during their English class.

"Yes, dumb wog?" he replied.

The boy stood up from his chair in the middle of class pounding his chest.

"Sit down please!" the teacher said.

Crash! My friend's books propelled across the room after his table flipped upside down.

Ridiculously the teacher escorted everyone else outside.

"Come on guys, lets leave them to talk things out," he said.

Highly unpredictable, the European was not someone you wanted to be left alone with. One time in electronics class I watched him place the tip of his soldering iron over its power cable, which was still plugged into the AC point. Hiding under the table with fingers in my ears I still heard the explosion. He never got into trouble for that however luckily for my friend, his situation escalated to the principal before getting hurt.

I'll never forget one time waiting at the bus stop outside school as a lowered commodore pulled up inside the bay. I felt chills at the sight of a girl hopping out wearing ripped tracksuit pants and a baggy shirt. I recognised her. She was a previous student at the school with a face that meant business. Strutting towards us with an anonymous male driver, another girl waiting with us for the bus hid behind another student clutching her schoolbag. From behind a bin I watched punches thrown, flying bags and heads colliding against the bus shelter glass. Pupils dilated, anyone that tried to break up the girls was left to deal with the stocky driver.

"You fucking bitch, I'm going to fucking kill you!" she said.

No idea what the fight was over but the memory of watching it unfold has stayed with me.

CHAPTER FOUR

FOR ME HIGH school was a roller-coaster. The days of work, study and tests seemed far more enjoyable than the days filled with socializing. My communication was limited through a means of saying "yes", "no", asking work related questions and making the occasional immature joke. General chit-chat felt unnatural and required too much effort, which made me choose to stay very quiet, only livening up around a small handful of other introverted boys. Looking back now I've come to learn there were many times at school I was masking. That is camouflaging certain traits in my behavior or speech to fit in. I will describe this in more detail later.

Peter was an exception in our friendship group. He could talk to anyone. I would watch with amazement how natural it was for him to talk to other students, not only from our year level but all levels. Boys, girls, parents and teachers it didn't matter who they were Peter could always relate.

"That boy can talk himself out of a brown paper bag," mum would say.

Everyone knew who Peter Coobey was because whenever he walked past, he smiled, waved hello and greeted with their name. I don't know how on earth he remembered them all. With the exception of memorizing Al-Qaeda, names are one area I've never excelled at. When walking alongside Peter's shadow I'd often ask how he knows that person. Every time he would answer convincingly, "We're best mates."

Back then my gullible self always believed what he said verbatim. It wasn't until years later after finishing school when I started to catch on.

Peter's popularity served him well when Egan High needed to select their next school captain. I remember one lunchtime discussing the voting for student leadership council. He was one of the short-listed nominees. "Lads, when you're doing your cards, make sure you put a one next to my name."

"Not again! You've been telling us this all week," I replied.

We were all barracking for him. He was the perfect man for the job. Our lunchtime discussion came to a standstill as everyone's eyes wandered when Scott walked past, carrying his new toy.

"What's that?" Peter said.

"My PC tablet, my parents bought it for me because I'm their favorite child," he replied.

He pulled out a pen and began touching the screen. We rolled our eyes. He was the only student carrying one. They were expensive (retailing around $1000) and weren't needed as the school had its own computer labs.

"Who are you voting for?" Peter said.

"I'm not voting for you because your dad works for Plascom," Scott replied.

We all laughed except for Peter.

"At least my dad drives a company car," he said.

Scott immediately refuted. "My dad can drive company cars if he wants, BMWs."

I remember Peter's eyes turning dark. Plascom was the plastering company his father worked for. Scott's father had his own plastering business, so the pair had this constant verbal battle during school on whose dad was more successful. I would often see Peter get very worked up, cursing under his breath about it at times, even in Scott's absence. Ever since the apple incident the two had it in for each other. I remember Scott blatantly threw an apple at full force, hitting Peter in the chest. He retaliated, charging at him like a raging bull, almost knocking him flat on his feet. We all thought he was going to put him in hospital that day.

All my mates had our share of beef with Scott. Whether it was for being a nerd, being Asian, partially deaf or uncoordinated at sports Scott verbalized it at every opportunity.

As the years progressed, I was hopeful Scott would mature and grow out of his verbal taunts. By the time we reach year 12 aside from the bus trips, we didn't run into each other as often. Fortunately, he wasn't enrolled in any of my chemistry, physics or advanced math classes and instead chose to study Media, Humanities and Outdoor Education.

However there was one day I will never forget. I'd decided to take a detour and walk a longer route to class. From a young age I've always enjoyed time in solitude, spending hours in my bedroom after school studying and listening to music by myself, refusing invitations to watch television with my family. I even insisted having a lock installed on my bedroom door so I couldn't be disturbed.

At times I enjoyed walking by myself, especially to recover after a busy lunchtime of socialising. Heading for the stairs a flurry of wind passed my face before I cringed at the scent of tobacco.

Suddenly my heart paused as my flight or fight response kicked in. Scott had his left hand inside his girlfriend's pocket, while the right held half a cigarette.

I tried to walk back down but it was too late. The peaceful surroundings soon became louder.

"Travy! Where's your girlfriend Travy, hey, hey, hey Travy."

I looked up at his brown eyes as he smirked. His girlfriend

grabbed the cigarette from Scott's hand then laughed, indicating she knew something was about to happen.

Leaning against the handrail, I acknowledged them with a nod but before I had the chance to say hello, Scott's free hand punched me in the shoulder. I flinched, then arching back, his hand continued over my right arm, which was carrying my pencil case and books.

Scott's girlfriend's hair curled in the wind. "Stop, he's probably gay," she said.

Whenever I saw her, she appeared genuinely interested in Scott, which always had me baffled.

I remember scrambling across three treads, bending over for my items. With one fingertip on my pencil case Scott booted it away like an American football kicker. We all heard the snap when his foot made contact with my graphics calculator inside the pencil case. I shrieked in horror before chasing it, hoping to catch it before it landed. Crash! They both cackled.

"Goal!" Scott said.

Just when I thought my situation had improved, I had gone back to square one. Sadly my calculator had a cracked screen and died the following day. I was gutted. Back then calculators were similar to what mobile phones are today. Mine had programmed games, mathematical charts as well as the periodic table of elements. I had saved up $200 of my own money and purchased it myself. Maths classes weren't the same again.

CHAPTER FIVE

I NEVER TOLD anyone Scott had destroyed my calculator. Looking back now I should've gone straight to a teacher or even the coordinator, however it meant speaking up which was something I didn't know how to do. At the time all the teaching staff were preoccupied with the news story unravelling in the background.

I remember having trouble concentrating during class where my head filled with insecurities. I would question myself on why Scott continued to pick on me and why it irritated me so much. At the time I also questioned if I was actually gay and how would I know for sure.

Interestingly both during and after high school my mannerisms observed by some people have been perceived as feminine, making them question my sexuality. Hearing this enough had me thinking if I should come out of the closet. Luckily I never did because little did I know I was never in a closet to begin with. I finally figured this out years later.

Scott was one of many troublemakers in our year level. Laying low I was able to stay clear of all of them except for one. Bart Osbourne.

I remember talking with Peter one time in the corridor when we were suddenly caught off guard by his penetrating voice.

"I reckon you'd be a good root!" he said.

Several bystanders looked at me, waiting for a response. I blushed as everyone around laughed.

"I think he's giving you a compliment," Peter said.

Bart Osbourne peacocked past with his army of jocks. Moreso than Scott, he wasn't the type of person I wanted to be around. Luckily Bart was never in any of my classes. I only saw him appear when wolf whistling to girls down the corridors and singing the inappropriate lines of songs, emphasizing the swear words. "Oh yeah, give me a fuckin sign, hit me baby one more time!" Bart's version of the Britney Spears classic hit.

Our first conversation wasn't until year 10 at the athletics carnival when he confronted me at the 200m starting line.

"You do realise my mum held the record for the 200m," he said

I looked up from my crouched position and smiled. "That's nice."

His eyes widened as the steam dissipated from his head, then coming within an inch of my face he roared. "That's fuckin awesome!"

Whether hardened from a broken family or losing his virginity at a young age, Bart was perceived as a confident force no one wanted to mess with. Chest out, he would have no shame ramming you into a wall if you looked at him the wrong way.

If there was a hierarchy of power, Bart had total access to the throne and would be hailed king. Over time as the troublemakers either dropped out or were expelled, no one else could challenge him. For reasons I still don't understand this allowed him to say and do whatever he pleased, terrorising law-abiding students like myself.

I'll never forget the Egan High Awards Night. I didn't want to go. Being in the same room as Bart or Scott wasn't my idea of a good time. In the end it was Peter's enthusiasm, lifting me over the line.

"We're getting a limousine!" he said, excitedly.

Inside the fancy racecourse, we all assembled around a wooden board checking our names. Brushing past in my black slacks and white collared shirt, I read my name and nearly fainted. Bart and I were on the same table. Losing balance, I held onto a friend's arm after standing on his toe.

"It must be a mistake!" I said.

My friend laughed. "See if you can move."

Scanning the layout, I noticed there were eight names under each of the tables except for one which had only six. I immediately hunted down the coordinator and asked to be moved.

"That's the teacher's table, but I'll see what I can do after entrée," he said.

I remember my anxiety soon kicked in and I wanted to leave but our limousine had already gone. Sitting on a table with none of my mates was hard enough, but sitting on a table with Bart would be unbearable. After what happened the previous month, I wanted to avoid him at all costs.

Sliding between the curtains I circulated the table like a hawk, scanning name cards. Three people sat between Bart and me. Before I had a chance to switch my card a waitress interrupted,

"Excuse me sir, you can't be in here yet," she said.

I froze while trying to think of how to respond.

"Where's the bathroom?" I said.

The waitress frowned, pointing to the exit.

I remember sitting quietly looking across at Bart's empty seat. Everyone had arrived except for him then suddenly he stormed in with his hands up to his chest, both index, middle and pinkie fingers pointed out, ring fingers and thumbs folded down. His mates applauded as he chanted, "Two in the pink, one in the stink!"

Only years later did I realise what he'd actually meant.

I looked across the table at his red cheeks while he was greeted like a celebrity. Bart smirked, passing a golden hip flask to someone underneath the tablecloth.

After Peter's welcome speech, the noise lifted as people moved around the room. Before I had a chance to get up a creepy hand grabbed my knee. He whispered into my ear. "Hey Travy!"

I remember leaning back in my seat, tensing my abdominals to stop wetting myself. I can still feel the hot air from his mouth and smell the musty alcohol causing my body to seize. Everyone else was too preoccupied to notice Bart had moved across three seats. His hand tightened grip.

"Piss off!" I said.

In his leather jacket and maroon shirt, he rubbed my knee. My bottom lip trembled listening to his gurgling sounds. I shifted my body to the other side of the seat, then felt the pressure of his hand move toward my crouch.

"Enough!" I said.

Without even laying an eye on him I carried my chair across the dancefloor, heading for the furthest table away. That was the second time in two months I felt sexually violated by him. I remember pushing someone's cutlery aside with a sense of urgency. A girl on the table pulled a bitchy face.

"What are you doing?" she said.

Once she found out what happened, she was shaking her head with disgust. She then shared a story on how Bart made an offensive comment one time after she offered the class a round of cakes for her birthday. Bart stuck out his tongue in her direction, flapping it up and down.

"Can I have some of your muff for dessert?" he said.

CHAPTER SIX

SCOTT AND BART were never reprimanded by the teachers, so it left them a taste for wanting more. Like when an animal in the wild builds a thirst for the blood of its prey. They were hunters and I was their source of food.

Laying low at school became increasingly difficult at times. "Hey Travy, you've been acting differently lately," Scott said to me in class after our Italian teacher left the room. Then looking around to ensure others were tuned in. "Your parents must be going through a divorce!"

I remember my face turning a hot red, pressing my lips together as I sucked in the embarrassment. Somehow, he had found out my parents (likely through his own parents) had been arguing after my dad lost his driver license for drink driving. I wanted to get up and wipe the grin off his face.

Dad blew 0.14 (three times the legal limit) into a breathalyser and had been riding a bicycle and hitching rides with mum to get to work. The extra time spent commuting us children to and from weekly activities had created tension. It was a difficult time in my family which twenty other students found out from Scott's big mouth.

Aside from his mouth Scott had picked up another interesting trait. He walked around school with a notorious gait. With each step he took long strides, causing his body to bob noticeably more than everyone else. It almost looked forced, making me question whether it was because of his long legs or if he was trying to strut.

Years later I found out he had a desire to be accepted from Bart and his fellow jocks, desperate to belong to their group. This explained a conversation I overheard one day when one of the jocks received praise. Apparently, he was a hero after bleeding from watching porn and pulling himself too hard.

"I've done that three times before!" Scott said.

He was trying to impress and wanted to be just like them. But why? Why would anyone want to be like Bart? Had I understood this at the time I may not have retaliated the way I did.

Not once did I ever feel the need to belong with any of the jocks. They were bad news. Most of them picked fights. I remember in year 9 one of them tried to recruit me for an organized fight between the wogs and the skips. The wogs being anyone of European and/or darker decent and skips being the white Caucasian Australians. Once I found out the day it was going down, I called in sick. Egan High was also banned from playing rugby against other schools because the jocks in our year caused too many fights. I know one boy from my year level who is still reminded of his mistake every time he looks in the mirror. The scar extending from his eye down to his mouth is still visible decades after taking a glass bottle to the face.

One of the main reasons I bought bolt cutters was for protection. They had been sitting underneath my bed untouched for over a year and were more of a sense of feeling safe. At the time I told myself I would only ever pull them out if necessary. Peter had also forgotten the day when I made the purchase and let's be honest, I was far too chicken to cut anything. Or was I? It's crazy what happens sometimes when the straw breaks the camel's back.

I often wondered how my younger siblings coped with bullies

at Egan High. My sister Eleanor was in the year below and my brother Jack started the year after. I don't recall ever hearing problems however in saying that their cohorts were smaller in size and likely far more level-headed.

Jack was a hyperactive child who seemed to have no fear in high-risk behaviours such as climbing trees, climbing the walls inside our house, walking over ants' nests in bare feet and playing with broken glass. During his primary school years he had problems obeying my parents, often defiant and arguing with them, regularly getting himself into trouble. Admittedly I also used to push his buttons and watch with delight when he became emotionally worked up and physically lash out.

I remember our visit to the doctors one time. Mum gave us her car keys and asked Jack and I to wait inside while she sorted out the bill with reception. I sprinted to the car, quickly jumping in before locking the door.

Jack banged the bonnet and screamed with volcanic temper.

"Hey! Let me in!" he said.

I shook my head and laughed with a cheeky grin.

It didn't take much for Jack to pick up a handful of rocks and begin throwing them at the windows with aggression. I remember closing my eyes and ducking for cover behind the seat as the glass began to crack.

Mum was horrified when she returned to the car that day. Jack had obliterated two of the windows. I'm sure the cost to replace them far outweighed the doctor's bill.

For the following week Jack was sent to bed at 5pm every night before dinner. I remember watching him mope through his bedroom window while the rest of us were allowed to ride bikes and play around outside on a sunny day.

But by the time Jack reached Egan High, he seemed to quieten down and mature. He got better with age. Unlike myself who seemed to get worse.

They say the oldest child tends to be more responsible, ambitious, and conscientious taking on the role of a leader, thereby setting a good example for their younger siblings. This couldn't be farther from the truth as you'll soon discover in the following chapters.

CHAPTER SEVEN

I CAN STILL hear the bang of the sliding door bashing against its stopper.

We all stopped as three characters stormed inside the classroom, one of which wasn't wearing any pants. Out of the corner of my eye, I saw Peter and the others look at me with concern. He lowered his underwear.

"Travy! Look at my cock," he said, stressing the word "cock".

I turned the opposite direction, out the window. In the company of his two giggling jock followers, I should've fly kicked him in the groin, but I was too scared.

My arms tensed, gripping the bottom of the seat as Bart stood over me, repeating the above phrase like a military general. I remember he fiddled with his genitals like they were play-do, moving things around to make the shape of a hamburger. My mates all watched in fear.

"Leave him alone," one of them said.

"Shut up!" one of the jocks replied.

Due to the unpleasant mix of his deodorant and body odour, I covered my nose. "No! Piss off!"

Every time I refused his voice became more aggressive. I wish I had the courage to look him in the eye.

The volume lifted as Bart dragged me up off the chair. Like a dog about to enjoy a meal, the saliva reflected off his chin hair.

After some pushing and shoving, his thicker frame overpowered, pinning me against the wall. Then trapped inside a bearhug, I felt his lumpy pelvis stab against my backside.

The jocks egged him on, watching with enjoyment until one of them pounded the alarm. "Teacher!"

Their laughter came to a stop when someone offered Bart his pants. The three retreated as I stared helplessly at the ground. My friends shook their heads in disbelief. It was the most horrendous experience of my high school life. What Bart did to me that day was far more malicious than anything Scott had ever done. I can still vividly recall details of the incident. Bart's grand entrance, the classroom location, time of the day, year and specific words from his mouth. I wish I could forget but my long-term memory just won't allow it.

"That was sexual harassment, you should tell the coordinator," one of my mates said.

Peter nervously touched his sternal notch. "Are you ok mate? He shouldn't have done that,"

I remember someone handing over my glasses which had a broken arm after being knocked off my face. Watching everyone's feet crowd around I embraced the army of support. With my head down too embarrassed to speak, I contemplated on what to do. It is here when I should've listened to my mate's advice and gone straight to the coordinator, but at the time I was too blown away and didn't know what to say. I remember thinking what I would tell the coordinator, "Excuse me sir, Bart Osbourne just tried to root me". How would it go down? I didn't think he'd believe it, and if he did, he'd be too weak to punish him properly. I had lost faith in the teachers at Egan High. Too many of them failed to address the reality of what went on. I couldn't trust them. Especially with the rumours floating around during the time of the Bart incident.

There was talk a boy from my year level was sleeping with one of the teachers. I never believed it until the day it turned out to be true. And surprisingly it wasn't Bart. Dirty Dean, one of the jock followers was having a secret relationship with Miss Petrova. Two police cars had arrived one day and took them both into custody.

Most of the boys liked Miss Petrova because she was young and attractive. Everyone gawked whenever she walked past, taking in the smell of her fruity perfume and the appearance of her glittering lipstick. When she spoke, everyone listened, even the disobedient ones who'd get kicked out of other classes. One time I got a hard on when I saw her at school wearing a loose crop top on a 30-degree day. I remember pulling my shirt down so I could tuck it in. I was totally shocked when I heard about the allegations. I didn't think any teacher would be so foolish and remove their clothes around a 17-year-old on school property.

Two of our teachers were sacked for knowing about the affair and not reporting it sooner. Given the unravelling media hype, the school was approaching its tipping point, staff were worried for their jobs, which sadly took priority over disciplining troublemakers such as Bart.

CHAPTER EIGHT

SOMETHING INSIDE ME snapped. I remember the day my body shook with burning rage which seemed impossible to fend off. It was like the incident with Bart had blown a fuse inside my brain, turning any positive thought into a negative. When trying to think about something happy such as family, sport or schoolwork, my mind could only fixate on getting even. The line had been crossed and I needed to respond. I wish I'd shared these thoughts with a teacher or my parents at the time because I needed help. I was helpless. Looking back there was a mountain sized problem in front of me which felt impossible to climb. My undiagnosed conditions made it all too hard, steering me in the wrong direction.

Scott and Bart pranced around school doing whatever they pleased without repercussions. It was going on for too long and someone needed to teach them a lesson. This led me to what I believed at the time was the only remaining option. I was to become a vigilante and seek justice. An eye for an eye as they say! And if I could get creative and punish them both without anyone knowing, there would simply be no need to talk about it. No one would know it's me. I truly believed I was doing the school a large favour for everyone who got picked on. I would be their hero! It all made perfect sense. I pushed aside my schoolwork and vigilantism soon became my special interest.

One day after school I sneakily made my way into one of the toilet cubicles and hid, waiting for everyone to head home.

I remember blocking my nose from the scent of urine and nervously ran over all the potential failures in my head i.e. What if someone sees me? What am I going to say? What if I get caught?

The back of the cubicle door was covered with graffiti and permanent marker. Someone had drawn a big set of boobs and written, "If you want to suck on these, call 6789998212". I still wonder if it was actually a real number.

Pressing my ear against the cold wall I waited for the rushing footsteps and chatter to settle down. The door squeaked shut as I peered around the corner making sure the coast was clear.

I remember tiptoeing down the corridor like I was Tom Cruise from Mission Impossible. Passing the Italian and Japanese noticeboards my feet felt like they were walking on hot coals.

Our school building had vinyl flooring that shone against its brick walls. The ceilings sat low, and I can recall many of us jumping up to touch it over the years. There were many windows running along the corridor however all were tinted and didn't allow visibility from the outside.

As you can see in the picture this area of the school housed the lockers for not only my year level but also the year below which happened to be my sisters. Eleanor was different to me. I'd see her at school hanging around the popular kids, laughing

and holding hands with different boys. On weekends she'd go out underage drinking at house parties, while I either worked at my casual supermarket job or stayed home in my bedroom either studying or watching The X-Files on TV.

As different as we were in personality, years later we discovered a fascinating commonality between us. Something most siblings around the world would never even know.

The corridor was dead and the only sounds I could hear were from me. They felt amplified. I remember taking a deep breath wanting to chicken out but the thought of being abused again kept me moving forward. With every bit of strength, I opened the bolt cutter jaws, then positioning over Scott's padlock, three, two, one.

The sound ripped like a tidal wave. I can still feel my body stiffen into a statue waiting for any response from the classrooms. My heart pounded wanting to run away, but I forced myself to soldier on.

My objective that day was to sift through Scott's locker and steal his calculator after the damage he did to mine. It was only fair. I also desperately needed a new one for maths.

Pushing aside the cricket magazine and boxing hand wraps I remember pausing at his Parramatta tin. One time he changed teams halfway through the season, buying an Eels guernsey when they started dominating the competition. When others engaged in rugby conversations, he would say in his powerful voice, "Sorry guys but all your teams except for mine are shit."

I also recall his Chopper pencil case. Given the same surname Scott had an interest with the famous criminal, often blurting lines from the movie. One of his favorites was, "I'm just a bloody normal bloke who likes a bit of torture."

Behind an empty Coca-Cola can I saw a black pouch which looked like a cover for a calculator. With a short burst of energy, I opened it up only to find his PC tablet. I sighed with disappointment dropping my chin to my chest. In moments of panic, I could only focus on searching for his graphics calculator. It wasn't until I'd emptied out his entire locker when it finally registered. I had something even better. Scott's tablet would certainly have an in-built calculator application. Eureka!

Wasting no more time I tucked it safely away and left the schoolgrounds like a bat out of hell. To my knowledge, not one person saw me enter or leave that day.

CHAPTER NINE

I BROKE INTO Scott's locker on a Thursday. Thursday was the day I visited my grandfather. On my way home I would pass by his house before my weekly running sessions. He always had pre-prepared a delicious roll smothered with mashed banana. Sometimes he'd forget to mash it and I'd be opening my mouth far and wide to fit it in.

On that Thursday, I sat down at the kitchen table and took Scott's PC tablet from my rucksack. It was surprisingly lightweight. While I was eating and playing around with it, grandfather peered over my shoulder and asked, "What have you got there?"

"Um, a new calculator for school," I replied.

"Can it cut one from the herd?" he replied.

I raised my eyebrows. Before I had a chance to ask what he meant he began singing, "Oh, Danny boy, the pipes are calling."

He then stood up from his favorite chair holding a beer. I watched with interest as he dropped a small piece of brick into his glass. It made a fizzing sound similar to soluble Panadol in water. He believed the brick increased the head (froth) of the beer, making it taste better. My grandfather was certainly a man with a high regard for beer, almost as much as his son (my dad).

I'll never forget the time he faceplanted at our family friends' house. He fell down a step while drinking his glass of beer. Somehow, he was able to turn his body enough to avoid spilling any on the carpet.

On his way to the hospital with a broken arm he proudly said to the paramedic, "I never spilt a drop!" I often think back even if it was milo, I'd much rather drop it on the floor instead of quibbling around home for two months in a sling.

Once my grandfather turned on the radio and placed his daily bets on horse races, his interest with Scott's tablet was gone. Like his son my grandfather also had poor money management skills. At the time I was more worried about my parents finding Scott's tablet, particularly mum who regularly cleaned my bedroom.

When I arrived home that evening, I snuck into the backyard accessing the door underneath our balcony staircase. Crawling along the dirt I found a safe place for the tablet behind a pile of rubble. After dusting off the cobwebs tickling my skin, I went inside to join my parents for dinner.

"What does cutting one from the herd mean?" I said.

My dad bellowed with laughter almost knocking over his pewter mug. It was a present for his 21st birthday which he used most nights of the week. The brim of the mug had many indentations and even a thumbprint in the metal from all his years of drinking.

Once realizing what my grandfather's question meant, I blushed. Herd had referred to girls (not sheep) and I was supposed to be their farmer.

I remember the next day at school camouflaging myself behind students, watching Scott's hot face from afar speaking with our coordinator. Stance stooped, he pointed at the open locker firing questions. I couldn't hear exactly what was said over the noisy corridor and the sea of people crowding around but you could tell he was upset.

I was worried, not only for getting caught but also for what might happen to me if I was found out. I didn't know how our coordinator would handle the situation because he wasn't very disciplinary. Mr. Zoltan was seen as a nice guy and had a reputation of being a pushover. Whenever he spoke to students, every sentence ended with the word "please" so many of us, especially the jocks never took him seriously. He was also shorter than most of them too! I look back now and feel sorry dragging him into the mess. With everything else going on at the time I'm sure the last thing he wanted to deal with was stolen property.

Over the coming days at school, I didn't hear much about Scott's missing tablet. No rumours, no questions from teachers or announcements demanding anyone to come forward. The uncertainty of it all made me quite edgy. So much that I remember giving into my urges and fishing for more information. "Hey, I heard something happened to Scott's…"

Peter cut me off. "Yeah! The coordinator questioned me about it."

I leaned in. Everyone else stopped eating.

"Someone nicked Scott's tablet from his locker, they think it happened after school hours," Peter said.

I unwrapped my muesli bar while listening attentively to every detail. Being mates with Peter was a real bonus. After he was awarded the role of school captain nothing got past him. He spoke with Mr. Zoltan every day!

"I'm supposed to be reporting back suspicious behaviour, but I don't care for that little shit," he said.

My friends muttered their displeasure.

"They asked me too," Allan said.

Shy and lean Allan was one of the regulars spending time with us during breaks at school. He rarely opened up, so no one really knew much about him. Most of his conversations were either surface level or humorous when joining in with Peter for impersonations. The two of them would drift off into their own little world imitating silly things about mates, teachers, television celebrities and football stars. Sometimes I'd try and join but could never keep up with their speed. It would take me too long to figure out which person they were talking about.

"Have they looked at the cameras?" Allan said.

Hearing him ask a question in his regular voice got my attention. As I swallowed, a piece of muesli bar went down the wrong pipe. My eyes watered and I coughed. A thick arm wacked me behind my shoulders.

"Are you ok mate?" he said.

I still remember the moment Allan's question freaked me out thinking it was only a matter of time before I'd be dead meat. I felt faint as the blood rushed through my body. The whole time I had no idea there were cameras inside the building and the thought of it didn't even occur to me. They kept talking as I lifted my eyes up to the ceiling for anything obvious.

Rather than asking them where the cameras were I panicked, worrying I'd be in the running for a Hollywood oscar.

I turned around making sure no one else was nearby, then took a deep breath. I needed to know everything there was about these cameras. I needed their help, so I confessed.

"I know where Scott's tablet is!" I said.

Peter scratched his head. "Huh?"

"I stole it."

Everyone paused, looking at me like stunned mullets.

"How?" Allan said.

Peter covered his mouth in shock. "Do you still have those bolt cutters?"

I had trouble filling them in without being interrupted. Although blown away with disbelief, by the end everyone appeared to understand. Noone felt pity for Scott. From all the years of his accumulating abuse, supporting me appeared to be an easy decision for them. Even though I had unintentionally dragged them into it we were all in this together.

CHAPTER TEN

I LOOK BACK now and laugh at how foolish I was. Not only did I steal Scott's tablet, but I also told three mates about it. That's three mouths whom I needed to trust and keep the secret. Any slip of the tongue or miscalculation could potentially throw us all under the bus and jeopardise our graduation from high school. It's hard enough staying silent as an adult with diagnosed ADHD let alone an undiagnosed 17-year-old schoolboy. And given how popular and well-respected Peter was there was a lot at stake.

After school I pulled Peter aside. "Are the cameras turned on?" I watched him ponder for a moment.

"Let's find out!" Peter said.

I now realise his pause indicated reluctance to get involved.

We looked up at the corridor ceiling. Hand on his chin Peter examined the corner piece which abutted two glass double doors. The doors were one of only two entrances into the building.

Whether the cameras were actually working or not I still remember the extreme agitation from the thought of being recorded. So much in fact I skipped school one day to visit the hairdresser, changing my appearance and dying my hair brown. Back then I was desperate and prepared to do anything. Interestingly it solved my bee problem. One of the downsides with red hair is that bees hover around your head thinking you're a flowering plant with pollen. Kiel tells me this is just an urban legend.

It wasn't until after two weeks of laying low and taking a few sick days from school when Peter shared some relief.

Apparently, he had raised the issue about the security cameras at the monthly school council meeting. Being the chairperson gave him the power to find out information, liaise with the principal and get things done around the school.

I remember he approached me on the basketball courts in his new blazer.

"Nice hairdo," Peter said.

I smiled, then squinted from the sun reflecting off his captain badge.

"Jeez you're fucking lucky," he said.

I felt like a tonne of weight was lifted off my shoulders, however for some reason Peter still looked worried. "There's two security cameras in the building, they're not recording, but now since the missing tablet they want to get them working again."

It was clear my actions had prompted a response from the school and that what I'd done meant something. I remember at the time feeling kind of special, like something I'd done had actually made a difference. Even if it was bad. I guess it must have been how Scott and Bart felt after bullying me all those years.

Running his hands through his black hair, Peter subtly pointed out the two camera locations. There was one camera at each end of the long corridor. I remember they were directed over the locker area and passageway but only viewed as far as the middle of the building.

Peter wiped away a drop of sweat falling down his face then asked me a question which to this day still has me baffled.

"Hey, can I borrow the tablet?" he said.

I stepped back and raised an eyebrow. I really wanted to say no.

Not only had I been using it as a calculator but lending it to him was extremely risky. At the time Peter explained he needed to use it to help with his study because he was falling behind.

Before I had a chance to give him an official answer we were joined by Erika.

Erika was a voluptuous blonde from the year below Peter had been paying special attention to. She was also related to our principal Mr. Sheffield, but I couldn't see any resemblance. She was attractive however her looks quickly faded as soon as she opened her mouth. She had a scratchy high-pitched voice and spoke with foul language using phrases like "son of a bitch" and "motherfucker" which were painful to my ears. Not Peter's ears though. He enjoyed the flirting games and the attention she was giving him.

I still remember the first time Peter introduced us.

Erika gave me strange look.

"Hello," I said.

She looked me up and down like I was an alien from outer space. Peter non-verbally probed her to respond.

"So does your carpet match the drapes?" she said.

Peter immediately turned red. He then rubbed the side of his head with his fingers. I had no idea what she was asking so I peered around in search for anything looking like carpet and drapes. If only we were standing inside a house my answer would've sounded more confident. At the time I replied with the tone of a question inflection. "Yes?"

She giggled like a cheeky toddler. It was a classic example of a literal interpretation. Something my autistic brain naturally gravitates towards in conversation. Over my life it has caused many moments of embarrassment and misunderstandings, and I can only look back now and laugh at times like this. For the record my answer wasn't a lie.

A month had passed since I took the tablet, and I wasn't even close to being caught. I was never questioned by teachers or even

Scott regarding the event, so it appeared breaking and entering into Scott's locker was surprisingly easy. I look back now and believe this gave me a sense of power. It was like I had a weapon to fight back, and if anyone tried to bully me again, I knew what to do. It gave me a purpose, something I had struggled to find at school. Inside my head I'd taken on the role of a secret vigilante, working hard to punish those who'd given others a hard time over the past. Let's face it the teachers weren't the best role models, so it was time someone stood up and took charge.

I believe it was simply the only way I knew how to deal with high school experiences. As hinted already social dynamics were difficult for me to understand. Sometimes the best way for me to interact was by being silly and making jokes in the hope people would laugh and enjoy my company. I remember when I was in year 10, I covered my mouth in yoghurt then walked around the schoolyard during recess pulling faces. Peter loved it and thought it was hilarious however my sister thought I was weird. Although her and I respected each other we didn't talk overly much during our school years. We were just different. For Eleanor's 16th birthday she convinced my parents to hold a party in our backyard. While roughly fifty people drank and smoked in our backyard, I spent the night inside watching the back to the future trilogy.

Back then getting away with Scott's tablet provided some feelings of achievement. And once something captivates me, it clings on for dear life making it extremely difficult to let go and focus on something else. Even today when having a conversation, brushing my teeth, having a shower or using the toilet my mind can wander and easily lock onto something else. It's like everything else in the world disappears. I've come to learn this is a neurodivergent trait called hyperfocus, which eventually moved away from Scott and shifted towards Bart.

CHAPTER ELEVEN

"MY MOUTH IS a bit sore; it must be from licking all that cunt," Bart said.

Of everyone who curiously turned, his deep eye sockets would scan the corridor before pinpointing my location. I often detoured around his locker area to avoid him, which worked well until the day I made a wrong turn.

"Get out of the way," I said.

He shuffled from side-to-side blocking my path. A few others watched with interest. Anytime Bart created a scene, people took notice of the entertainment.

My face cringed when he put his fingers inside his mouth. Retracing my steps I'd quickly turned 180 degrees but unfortunately on this day I wasn't quick enough.

"Gross!" I said.

My head sunk into my shoulders as I felt the sensation of his saliva-moistened finger twisting inside my left ear. The sloppy wet willy was one of his favourites. He'd target others as well, but most were able to escape before he had a chance to get his fingers inside.

By this point I'd had more than enough. Bart had crossed the line months ago and I simply had to respond. Deja-vu of the negative thoughts began to consume me once again. Something inside me just didn't sit right. I kept replaying past experiences over and over in my head. The discomfort, the shame, the abuse, I couldn't let it go. I remember at the time resonating with an INXS song I heard on the radio,

The devil inside,
The devil inside,
Every single one of us the devil inside.

Whenever I hear it again this song always takes me back to high school. Back when I thought everyone around me at school (including myself) was a devil.

Once again only one option remained on the table with Bart. I look back now and wish I could've seen the other options in front of me however at the time my brain could only focus on seeking justice and teaching Bart a lesson.

Peter shook his head assertively. "I wouldn't do that."

I remember one of my mates was biting on his fingernails, looking nervous. As did Allan and our other mate standing next to him. I had pulled them all aside and brought it up during our lunch break.

"You don't need to do it again, what if they find out about the tablet?" Peter said.

I looked over at Allan who was chuckling to himself. Over the years both him and I found Peter's comments humorous. I remember the time he told us he'd invited a well-known professional rugby player to his birthday. During the party when we asked him which one he was it happened to be a retired player who was working behind the bar at the venue.

I had handed over Scott's tablet to Peter a few weeks earlier which he said he needed for his Humanities studies. How he was using it I'm still not sure, but ironically Scott also took the same class. I decided to buy a second-hand calculator to get me through the year, so I was no longer reliant on the tablet.

"You can still return it later on, no one has to know," someone said.

Peter didn't flinch. Looking back now I think he was enjoying his new toy. Raising my head, I remember looking at the worried faces on each of the guys and having second thoughts. Alarm bells were signalling danger, but I was too committed to the plan to back out.

I remember us collectively brainstorming ideas on what I could possibly do to get rid of Bart and concluded in order to get rid of him I had to become him. I had to get inside his vulgar head. What is something he might do so bad, the principal would have no choice but to expel him. And once gone, no one at the school would ever again need to be traumatised by his absurd behaviour. I could be a hero!

After everything we plotted against Bart, Peter still looked concerned. He became more supportive when I assured him I'd take care of the cameras. At the time I simply needed to pay Bart back for what he'd done. He'd crossed the line many times and just like Scott, I needed revenge. There was simply no other way. Revenge had proven to be the most effective method to deal with bullying at Egan High. Since the day I broke into Scott's locker, he appeared to have quietened down, lying dormant. I remember whenever glancing at him from afar he looked rather wary of those around him, watching his back. At the time my acts of retaliation seemed to have worked. He hadn't dished out any abuse for months.

Taking into account everyone's input, I remember placing my hands on my hips like superman and ending with boldness. "Let's do this!"

In this moment I wish I'd listened more to Peter and considered pulling out because the next few months at school were about to take a nasty turn. Had I have known the situation would escalate the way it did I would've chosen a different path.

For Bart more work and planning needed to be done. Security cameras were now in operation and students and staff were on guard for any suspicious activity. I remember staying back after school one day to examine the ceiling of our building. The security cameras were tightly bolted inside a metallic shell casing which unless removed provided no access to any cables. There was only one way to stop them from recording which was to cover up the lens. Using a ruler, I jotted down the dimensions before sneaking into the art room for two sheets of black A4 cardboard paper.

Peter updated me on the coordinator's movements. Mr. Zoltan was an early riser, arriving well before first class then leaving abruptly at the end of each day. He would show me where his office was, where he stored certain documents and where he spent most of his time during school. I remember he also enjoyed showing me the Facebook profile of Mr. Zoltan's daughter who happened to be the same age as us. His pupils dilated. "She's attractive, look at her hair! Shit shoes though," he would say. I was never interested but always nodded, pretending to agree.

Allan subtly eavesdropped on conversations Bart had with his jock followers then filled me in on anything noteworthy. He was the polar opposite of Peter. No one at school really knew who he was, making him the perfect fly on the wall. Not that he had to try very hard. Bart word vomited anything and everything on his mind. But when anyone saw Allan at school, they'd assume he was a new student or someone unfamiliar from another year level. To this day Allan is still perceived as this cloak-and-dagger character. None of us quite know exactly what he does with his spare time. We don't know if he has a job or how he gets by day to day. Whenever we ask, he either trails off or changes the subject.

Most of the information he fed me centred around girls Bart had slept with, was trying to sleep with or students he wanted to bash up. There was one striking thing though which I remember providing the ultimate light bulb moment.

We both laughed with anticipation.

"Brilliant!" Allan said.

CHAPTER TWELVE

FOR AS LONG as I can remember I've always had sensitive hearing. When I was eight my mum had to pick me up early from a blue light disco because I couldn't handle the loud music and strobe lights. While running around with a packet of nerd candies a few of us were playing a game of tiggy before the world around me transformed into a terrifying darkness. Wandering through the room like a lost soul, the split seconds of flashing light weren't long enough for me to keep my eyes open. I was blind and deaf that night. The bass from the song, "Here's Johnny" by Hocus Pocus vibrated the basketball court like an earthquake and yanked at the inner hair cells of my cochlear. The sensory overload experience left me bawling my eyes out, traumatised and avoiding loud music venues for years to come. Fortunately, I now understand the science behind what was going on and can overcome these challenges.

For these reasons I never attended many parties during my school years, except for one. Scott's 18th Birthday. I remember he invited nearly everyone in our year to celebrate in his backyard at home. I didn't want to go but forced myself to make an appearance. The guys suggested going to the party would help rule me out for being a suspect. And if Scott saw me there, it would be harder for him to believe I stole his tablet. Peter said he would join me too but pulled out last minute. He has a history of doing this. Even after high school there was a time he ventured over to a nightclub to chase after a girl instead of joining us at my birthday, which was only located around the corner. Apparently, the girl was a former model, so I've forgiven him.

I remember exactly where Scott's house was. Our bus passed it every day. It was one of those houses you take notice of when heading out of town. His family owned a three-story brick veneer dwelling on top of a hill. It had a paved driveway with a well-maintained garden that surrounded a sign advertising his dad's plastering business. The house was on a large block with tall trees, which made it easier to distance myself at the party. I remember counting around 80 people from school but none I was close with. Moving between circles I was approached by a deep masculine voice. "Why are you drinking water?" He then handed me a vodka, lime and soda from the esky.

"I can't sorry, I'm driving tonight," I replied.

Everyone at school got excited by the opportunity to drink alcohol when underage. I was never interested, and it wasn't until after graduating when I finally finished my first beer. "Finish it!" Dad would say. I would scrunch my face at the horrible bitter taste thinking how on earth dad swallows this down every day. He would shake his head. "Well, you're not my son."

Scott's party was full of underage drinkers and smokers and none of the adults around seemed to care. I remember being shocked when I spotted Cameron pushing his way through the crowd in the kitchen, a beer in his hand.

I curled my lips. "What are you doing here?"

"Hey! Me and Scott are talking now," Cameron smirked.

He sipped his beer before drifting towards one of Scott's friends. We didn't talk much after that. It was weird and at the time I thought his behaviour was strange. From the early days of year 7 he had been picked on more than anyone for his Asian heritage. He also had a vulnerable personality, openly sharing his love for Pokémon, Harry Potter and Star Wars and like most of my mates, lacked self-confidence. Although I didn't believe he would side with Scott, I still felt incredibly worried he might make a mistake and spill the beans. Given he knew about the tablet I didn't want to stick around and find out, so I left the party shortly after. I would have been there for an hour and remember Scott was too drunk and preoccupied with his girlfriend to say hello. I left wondering if he even realised I was there.

After Scott's party something in Cameron changed. It was like he came out of his shell and his old introverted nerdy self had faded. He still hung around us sometimes at school but seemed to develop new friendships with other groups. I remember watching him from afar and marvel whenever he spoke to girls with a newfound confidence. I didn't know how he was doing it. During recess one day he filled us in on a conversation he overheard at the party.

"Scott might be leaving the school soon," he said.

Apparently, his parents had filed complaints with our principal, demanding to be compensated for the missing tablet and threatening to remove both him and his brother.

I swallowed hard as a shiver went down my spine. Things sounded like they were getting serious, and I remember being scared for what the principal might do. But I soon forgot all about it after hearing from Peter.

"I'm best mates with the principal," he said.

His confidence was reassuring. Even when I suggested we should return the tablet back to Scott somehow, he shook his head. "There's no need mate, it's ours now."

CHAPTER THIRTEEN

IT WAS A day I'll never forget.

Unscrewing the vent duct in my bedroom floor, I reached for what was the most gruesome thing I've ever done. From a young age I've had this natural flare to orchestrate gruesome pranks. In year 8 we had to dissect a sheep's heart in science class. While the teacher explained the different types of arteries, I happened to glance over at a girl's un-zipped pencil case while holding a mass of blood and oozing soft tissue. Back then I had a crush on her. She often sat in front of me in class and I'd gaze at her long ponytail. She also wore a gold necklace which shined against her tanned European skin. I still remember the only time we ever spoke.

"Hey, can I borrow your ruler?" she said.

I was too petrified to verbally respond and just handed over the ruler. The intention behind my prank was to get her to pay more attention to me. Looking back obviously not the most efficient way to do it. Luckily my mate stopped me before it was too late.

I remember driving to school incredibly early on a Thursday wearing tracksuit pants, a black Nike jumper and beanie. I was on a mission and nothing could stop me. Parking at the end of a no through road I saw the back gate was locked. Then folding up my collar and turning my face at the icy wind I dropped to my knees. Egan High had a renowned hole in the bottom of the fence for the troublemakers to use when wagging classes and escape to McDonalds. The principal knew about it but never bothered to have the fence repaired. I pushed my bag through before scuttling along on all fours like a soldier.

Within a minute I was peering through the double glass doors outside our building. And just like Peter had described the doors were unlocked. Apparently, the janitors opened up earlier on Thursdays to collect all the garbage bins.

Hands shaking in fear I extended towards the camera lens with a black paper cut out and some Blu Tac. I can still feel the muscles cramping around my knees when I was standing on a stool trying not to fall.

Right hand side, middle row, three columns from the end. I still remember exactly where Bart's locker was and could easily point it out to anyone, even today.

Like a cat burglar I tiptoed down the gloomy corridor before freezing outside the coordinator's office. Not a sound. Swallowing hard I looked left then right. The corridor was eerily still.

With a firm grip on my bolt cutters preparing to slash Bart's padlock suddenly my eyes widened. I scratched my head and remembered thinking whether he'd packed up early and emptied it out. Every locker in the building was tightly fastened with a padlock except for his. After opening his door, I laughed at the sight of all his items laying there in a pile of mess. There I was standing heavily armed to break in when in hindsight little effort was needed.

I remember pausing with curiosity when coming across some of the items inside Bart's locker. Sitting underneath an empty box of condoms was a magazine with a beachy blond lady on the front cover looking coy. She had one arm on her hip and the other was reaching for her underpants. When I tried to turn over to page two the magazine brought me to page seven, which showed two bare naked ladies putting their fingers in each other's mouths. Examining it more closely I realised some of the pages were missing and some of them were stuck together. At the time I thought it was the weirdest thing and didn't understand why Bart hadn't thrown it out. What good is a magazine if you can't see all the pages! I look back now and simply laugh at my young self. But things become more bizarre and what happened over the following few minutes will stay with me for the rest of my life.

Fitting myself with gloves I pulled out a plastic container. Then scrunching up my lips in an attempt to block the stench, I smeared all of Bart's books in my faeces. Lifting up piles and turning pages to get in between, I gave his locker the complete shitty makeover. I hummed to myself while painting a Picasso, drawing lines and cutting shapes, making sure I covered as much surface area as possible. To this day I can still picture the clockwise motion of my right hand pressing into the paper of his exercise books. I remember giggling like a toddler pasting over the pretty ladies in his magazine, digging deep into his pencil case and stuffing the soles of a pair of shoes. The tables had turned, I was in control and Bart had no idea. The high school version of myself relished every second of the moment feeling like a million bucks however the older and wiser version now sees this through a much different lens. Dropping your guts on someone's property no matter how bad the person, is not ok and I very nearly got caught doing it.

The doors creaked. "Holy shit!" I muttered under my breath. The most memorable moment of my high school life was suddenly interrupted. Balancing the open container, I watched the double glass doors swing open as a bald head appeared. I remember my heart dropped and anxiety levels kicked into overdrive as I scrambled to hide any evidence. It wasn't until his handlebar moustache powerwalked passed the covered-up security camera when it registered who it was.

Mr. Chemilio, a biology teacher who ironically interviewed me in year 10 on why I wanted to continue studying at the school. It was compulsory at the time since many students were dropping out. Why on earth he was at school so early that morning still has me perplexed.

Closing in quickly I searched for an escape route but there was nowhere to run.

I dived into Bart's locker and yanked the door closed as far in as possible. I remember my eyes rolled back into my eyelids, feeling dizzy from the durian-like odour. His footsteps got louder before slowing down.

"How are you going Travis?" he said.

Hiding my pale face, I half turned, keeping both arms at full length inside. My voice strained.

"Oh, morning sir," I replied.

Staring at a layer of faeces I heard him sniff. I remember my heart pounded against the locker jolting my whole body. His sniff didn't sound like one you would expect from a blocked nose but rather the prompt kind you make when a smell captures your attention such as coffee or a barbeque. Back then I remember mentally preparing myself thinking, this is it I'm a goner, but luckily he brisked past and didn't stop to ask any questions. Once he entered one of the classrooms, I rammed the locker door shut before uncovering the camera and bolting for the car.

My stomach churned with distress. Even though I made a clean getaway the fact that he saw me was a huge problem. The uncertainty of what he might do killed me, and I remember running over all the possibilities in my head. Did I look suspicious? Could he smell anything out of the ordinary or was it just a random sniff? Would he even remember our interaction? Once the news spread, Mr. Chemilio might join the dots then gossip with staff about our 7am interaction. Bart's reaction was also a concern and there was nothing I could do to stop it. There was no turning back.

I look back and reflect on the downtime I had in the car before starting school that day. My hands trembled from the anxiety around negative thoughts of worse case scenarios spiralling out of control. i.e. what the future might bring. It was a sheer case of catastrophising. I've come to learn this is a common trait among the neurodivergent community and is something I've battled with over time in a variety of situations. Of course, some more warranted than others.

In this scenario most would catastrophise after doing what I did that morning. But everyday things like vacuum cleaners, dogs, motorbikes, making a decision on what clothes to wear and what to order from a restaurant menu can sometimes become overwhelming and create catastrophic anxiety. This is because they are highly unpredictable with an infinite number of possibilities out of our own control.

CHAPTER FOURTEEN

"WHY THE FUCK would I shit in my own locker?" Bart said.

He wailed his arms and thumped the wall with an iron fist.

Thump! My ears pricked up. I remember cautiously entering and stopping for a looksie. It was like having front row seats to a theatre. Looking back, I wish I was smart enough to pull out my phone and press record. It was hard withstanding the laughter. Biting the side of my cheek my mouth inflated with air. I then coughed, relentlessly fighting the urge to look at the sea of people congregating around his locker.

I had gotten changed and arrived at school in full uniform, blending in with everyone else as they hopped off the bus. I remember wanting to go home but knew the fear of missing out on his first reaction would kill me.

Bart was bright red, punching his locker in fury while the coordinator stood behind him covering his nose. Someone walked past and poked fun.

"Did someone beat you to it?" he said.

Bart grabbed the boy's collar and barked with exasperation. "Shut up you fat fuck!"

I remember loving the moment when he got told off for his foul language. "It's about bloody time!" I thought. I never understood why it didn't happen more often. Aggressive and vulgar language amplified from his mouth every day.

Allan approached me, full of energy. "Was that you?"

I took him around a corner trying to keep a straight face.

"No one believes him!" he said.

Apparently, Bart had told everyone at the start of the year he was planning to shit in his own locker on the last day of Year 12.

I burst out laughing as Allan and I wrapped arms around one another. Wiping my face from tears of joy I said, "What a loser." It wasn't long before Peter found us.

"You're unbelievable!" he said, dipping his face into his elbow pit. Allan smiled, lost for words.

We joined a group who were bouncing off their toes with excitement.

"Teachers are getting arrested and Bart's locker is full of shit, this is the best week of my life!" one person said. Earlier in the week we found out the horrific news Miss Petrova was facing jail time.

"I think Bart pooped in his locker and forgot to flush," another person said.

Allan poked fun by making weird sounds, impersonating Bart doing his business. My chest ached from intense laughter before someone out of the blue turned to me and pointed, "It was you Travy, wasn't it?"

I remember my body froze into a statue as my toes gripped the floor. I looked over at Allan who had his hand over his mouth, pretending to cough. Unless it's obvious, I have never been good at telling when someone is joking or being serious. It was extremely difficult back then and it's still difficult today. There's a guy I currently work with who's regularly sarcastic and it takes me forever (sometimes never!) trying to figure out his intentions.

The face of this high school boy accusing me was dead cold. The kind of face you make when you're about to pounce. He spoke quick and sharp which I've come to learn is usually a signal the person is joking. At the time though I had no idea and believed he was pointing the finger at me for something I actually did. I remember inhaling with shock and wanting to respond but nothing came out. Luckily after a few seconds he dropped his pointer and broke the awkward silence.

"You're too innocent," he said.

My chest loosened with relief, not really knowing if he was referring to Bart's locker, Miss Petrova or something completely different.

The amusement at school continued as the stories of Bart's mysterious locker incident quickly spread. I'll never forget English class that day. I was sitting next to Peter reading a passage from Shakespeare's Romeo and Juliet when a discussion between two girls on the table behind us sparked my interest. One of girls was upset after hearing Bart's locker had been vandalised.

"He was targeted," she said.

Head down pen to paper, I pretended to look busy.

"It's because he's intimidating. Everyone knows he has a big cock."

My pen scribbled across the page as other students in the class reacted in awe. I couldn't believe she said the C word without even trying to tone down her volume. I guess she was like Bart and had no shame.

"Oh come on! We all know he didn't do it," she said.

Peter laughed and immediately turned around eager to join the conversation. I often saw him overly friendly with this girl during school and believe their friendship continued even after we graduated. They never dated but for some reason he enjoyed talking to her. I'll never understand why. I thought she was yuk. A few months earlier that same girl stood up in class and said, "The only reason people are talking about Schapelle Corby is because she's hot."

The girls Peter seemed to idolise never ever appealed to me. In fact, most of them I wouldn't go near with a 10-foot pole, even if I had one. But he would likely say the same about the girls I idolise! Peter's girls were either full of themselves, caked to the brim with makeup, unfriendly or spent too much time posting fake stories on social media.

On the day of the locker incident Bart was unsettled. You could tell from the way he moved around, scaring anyone who looked at him the wrong way. He had many enemies from different year levels, so I assumed I was the last person on his list of suspects. He was on a witch hunt and I remember him gatecrashing our lunch-time tennis ball game.

"I can't study right now because all my books are full of shit," he said, after someone mentioned exams.

Our game stopped as everyone stared. I waited for others to respond before even attempting to move. A few laughed but you could tell they were holding back. Bart's face was tense, which sent a shiver down my spine. Although clearly outnumbered, his demeanour remained rock solid. At the time I wish I had the courage to confront him, look him in the eye and say, "You deserved it!"

Later that afternoon my mind played tricks on me, believing Bart was following me down the corridors. I remember hearing heavy footsteps. Each step was hitting the ground louder than mine, indicating the person was likely bigger. Fighting the urge to turn around I changed directions at the corner, then with one hand pushing open the toilet door a man spoke with an assertive tone. "Excuse me, Travis." Immediately recognizing the voice, I felt the blood rush to my face. Mr. Zoltan crossed his arms.

"What time did you arrive this morning?" he said.

His brown eyes pierced down at me like daggers. In all my years at Egan High I'd never seen him so serious. I kept my hand in contact with the door while meaninglessly repeating his words. "What time did I arrive,"

"Just answer the question please," he said.

Hearing the flushing pipes behind the wall, the coordinator

took a step closer, repeating his question. I stuttered and made filler sounds before coming out with, "Whenever the school bus dropped us off, which was…"

"That's ok, never mind," he replied.

I took a deep breath watching him pivot quickly towards another student heading in our direction. He then asked them the same question. Thank God he believed me because lying has never been one of my strengths. It takes an incredible amount of effort for me to speak a lie. Most would say it's a noble character trait, but it's got me into trouble in the past, and I've needed to learn the hard way when and how to use it.

During one family Christmas celebration, I received a snake plant from my auntie. It was hideous and not even close to being on my wish list. By the age of nineteen most understand the need to pretend when to like something, show appreciation and say thank you for the gift.

"I don't like plants!" I said.

Whether it was the way I said it or the look of disgust on my face, it was years before I received another Christmas gift from my Auntie.

CHAPTER FIFTEEN

WHEN CLASSES OFFICIALLY ended I remember feeling a sense of relief, enjoying the eat, sleep, study and repeat routine away from school. The solitude environment at home calmed my anxiety and from here I believed life would be easier. There was no longer any need to face the bullies at school. I had survived the last day, making a lucky escape from Bart and Mr. Zoltan and honestly believed I'd gotten away with the misdemeanours. Over the following month all I had to do was study and sit my exams. Once finished I'd never have to worry about Egan High ever again. The finish line and freedom were looming.

I remember the dream quickly died from a startling knock on my bedroom door. I had locked myself away to memorise Shakespearean quotes on the eve of my English exam.

"Who is it?" I said.

"It's me," El replied.

I pondered, looking up at my clock. Dinner wasn't for another hour. Why would my sister be calling me? I thought. Aside from greeting each other with a hello and eating together with the family we rarely spoke. Not because we had any beef but as mentioned earlier, we were different characters. She spent most of her time chasing boys and gossiping on our home phone while I either exercised, studied or played the Nintendo. I can recall one time my parents refused to give her any pocket money when she surged the monthly phone bill over $1000.

When I opened the door, her face looked amused. The kind of face you make when wanting to tell someone a joke. The kind when you're laughing at it inside your head and anticipate the reaction before sharing.

"Did you do something to Bart's locker?" she said.

The question fired a bullet right through my chest, knocking the wind completely out of my lungs.

"He pulled me aside at school today, asking if I knew anything," she said.

My lips curled, struggling to believe the words I was hearing from her mouth. I leaned in while trying to stop myself from hyperventilating.

"He said you pooed in his locker, then told me to help him get it out of you."

At the time my first thought was, why is he hauling my sister into this? If he believed I was involved what's stopping him from asking me directly. Confronting, pushing, shoving, and inappropriately touching me certainly hadn't been a problem for him in the past.

"I told him it doesn't sound like anything you would do, but I'd ask," she said.

I remember attentively listening to all the details and holding myself back from jumping in. El sounded bewildered like she couldn't believe we were having this conversation.

Closing my eyes I shook my head. Then attempting not to give away any obvious signs I changed the topic.

"How do you even know who Bart is?" I said.

She gave a coy smile, then as the light reflected off her makeup she said,

"We hooked up at a party last year."

Pressing my lips together my mouth inflated with air. It was the only way I could stop myself from vomiting. Bart often taunted me at school for hooking up with my sister, but I never believed it was true. The thought of the two spending any time together at all made my skin crawl. Growing up I'd learned to push past my sister's poor choice in men. Most of them were large unkempt Aussie tradesman who thought highly of themselves. I'll never forget one guy who used to honk outside our house waiting for El to come out. Dad used to call him, "The Germ". Not once did he come inside to say hello. I'd wake up to the rattle of his truck whenever he'd drop my sister off in the early hours of the morning. In similar ways to Bart, he was also confrontational and recall a time he barked at me with aggression, "you can't talk, you have a big fucken gay question mark over your head!"

Not sure what El ever saw in these guys however if she finished up in a long-term relationship with either The Germ or Bart, I'd consider disowning myself from the family. Luckily for the record I can confirm it was nothing more than a party pash.

El primed her dark hair as curiosity got the better of her.

"So, did you do it?" she said.

Like a judge landing his gavel I replied, "No!" then after regaining composure I said, "Stay away from guys like Bart, he's dangerous! He pooed in his own locker, and now he's saying it's me to get out of trouble."

Eleanor nodded. "Yeah, makes sense."

I remember watching her walk away until out of sight. It didn't take much to convince her that day. Bart's reputation was enough for anyone to see he was his own worst enemy. Looking at things now maybe I was too. I hated lying to my sister's face but at the time I felt there was no other option. I needed El to think I was innocent so that when she spoke to Bart again, she would defend me with sincerity. If Bart found out it was me my life would be over. To this day I still have no idea why he went out of his way to speak to her.

After the conversation my anxiety levels elevated, and I had trouble sleeping. Lying in bed I moved back and forth like a rolling pin asking myself, does Bart actually think it's me or did someone tip him off? How? Why? Who else did he tell? Scott? The principal? Should I confess or keep denying it? It was a horrible preparation before the most important exam of my high school education. But things got worse. The next morning, I assembled outside our gymnasium with 150 other students gearing up for the exam. Keeping my distance alert for any hostility I remember seeing Bart wearing baggy trousers which had an unbuckled belt, causing them to sit low like a gangster. He looked around, showing no interest in the person talking to him.

I dropped my chin and turned away hoping he didn't see me, but I wasn't quick enough.

"Travy!" he said.

His voice echoed over the pre-exam chatter. There was no chance I could pretend not to hear. My knees trembled.

"Oh, hey mate," I said.

Standing well within my comfort zone he waited for me to elaborate. It was like he knew my sister had already spoken to me.

"What's this about your locker? My sister said something…"

"It was you, you're on the cameras," he said.

I tensed my jaw, trying to stop myself from smiling. It was then I knew he had nothing on me and must be following a hunch.

Staring at the bottom of his pasty face, I continued to play dumb while he interrogated me.

"You're the only person who would do it, no one else would," he said.

Then the scariest thing happened. As if Bart signalled him through a walkie talkie, Scott headed towards us. If the exam wasn't starting in a few minutes, I would've run away and wet my pants.

Bart gave Scott a smile. They didn't need to speak any words; their faces said it all. They had teamed up. The gymnasium doors opened as students began moving. Scott left to join everyone inside however Bart's feet were stapled to the ground. He didn't leave until I answered.

I remember digging for courage, taking a deep breath, then looking up into his brown eyes I said, "Sorry mate, it wasn't me." His face didn't flinch. I shrugged. "It wasn't me!" I repeated.

Bart hawked and spat on my shoes with authority. Immediately stepping around I made a run for the door. I was lucky he didn't grab me. Who knows maybe I convinced him just enough that day to avoid going to hospital. Back then I knew it wasn't over for him. He would come back for more.

I remember some time passed before Bart entered halfway through exam reading time, looking confused. He didn't stay too long, unlike myself who stayed until the very end. I often reflect had I not been shirtfronted before the exam my marks would have been far better. It was incredibly difficult shifting my focus from Bart back to writing about Shakespeare literature.

Bart aside, finishing exams within the required time frame has always been a challenge. I recall disappointment at times when forced to return my exam papers, before reading, comprehending and answering all the questions. If only we had the exam adjustment practices used in schools today where students with autism, ADHD and other disabilities are given the extra time they need.

CHAPTER SIXTEEN

PETER'S VOICE TURNED serious. "I need to tell you something." he said.

I blanky looked over at Allan who raised his eyelids.

"Bart is swinging past later to drop off some stuff." Peter said.

The veins surfaced on my skin. "He's what! Are you serious?" I replied.

"He had no room at the campsite," Peter replied.

Peter, Allan and I had gone away on a road trip down to Peter's beach house to celebrate finishing our final exams. We'd stayed in Palm Beach, a popular holiday destination about two hours north of Sydney. There were many other high schoolers in the area doing the same thing but I didn't think Bart would be one of them. Apparently, Bart had called Peter out of the blue asking for help. I still wonder what on earth he said to convince Peter to share his address. He knew what Bart was like. And of all the houses to stay he chose Peters. I remember thinking something was off and now regret my decision of not leaving when I had the chance.

I remember picking up my bag. "I'm going home," I said.

"No, stay!" Peter replied. Allan wasn't comfortable either.

I paced back and forth in procrastination before realizing Peter had the only car. His house was an hour walk into town and public transport was limited so I ended up biting the bullet and staying in. At the time Peter wasn't aware of the confrontation I'd had with Bart at our English exam.

Later on the windows rattled from the sound of bass when two cars pulled into the driveway. Peter went outside to open the gate while I hid underneath the bed. I knew it was him. It wasn't until I heard a tapping sound from the backyard when I finally came out.

Peter returned inside with a blushed face.

"What's going on?" I said.

He leaned towards Allan's ear and mumbled something I couldn't hear.

"Well?" I said.

"They're pitching tents, I said they can stay until they find another place."

I lurched forward in distress. "What! Are you nuts?"

"It's just one night," he said.

I threw my arms out. "Who's they?"

For reasons I still don't understand Peter allowed Bart and two of his jock followers to set up camp in the backyard. I was furious, questioning him several times on his thought process but he kept justifying his decision. As my mum mentioned earlier Peter had a gift of talking himself out of a brown paper bag. And his skills were on full display that day, persuading me not to leave. At the time I couldn't understand why he didn't persuade Bart and his followers. The house was no rental, it belonged to his family and he gave his consent for them to squat on their property. If his parents ever found out they'd ground him, probably forever if they knew the type of character Bart was.

For years I thought Bart must have either threatened Peter or paid him off. It's only now I look back and believe Peter was trying to seek approval and wanted to belong or fit in with Bart's group. Like many others at Egan High and even some people I deal with today it's all about perceived image. This is something I've never fully understood or ever prioritized for myself. Why would someone want to belong with a group who make life hard for others? And why do people like to be perceived in certain ways?

The situation got worse when none of our other mates came. One of them couldn't afford the trip and Cameron was unavailable. Peter had invited his cousin and his cousin's friend before saying the house was at full capacity. When I first heard they weren't coming I was disappointed. I'd lost two friends and gained three enemies.

I remember flinching when the back door slammed. We heard banter before Jimbo Jones entered the living room ducking his head. Closely behind him was Nelson cursing about the tents. I recognized the jocks straight away. They were notorious in our year level. Most of us thought of Jimbo as the gentle giant in Bart's group. With the face of a puppy, he was the happy go lucky type supporting whatever cause needed him. If he wasn't part of the jocks and hung around a different group, he would've been far more likeable. Who knows maybe we could've been mates. Nelson was far less welcoming and a better fit of the jock stereotype. He carried around a huge ego and had older brothers at Egan High which powered his cockiness. One time I watched the three of them take on a group of five jocks from the year below and had them bleeding within seconds. After being in Nelson's class during my early years I'm surprised he even finished school. He was the type to bicker with teachers with phrases such as, "Miss, when are we ever going to use this in life?" I felt sorry for our teachers having to put up with him.

Sitting on the couch I gripped the armrests, listening to their loud exchanges.

"Can I pay that with EFTPOS?" Jimbo said as Bart walked into the room shirtless. The other leaned his patchy head on the wall.

"Fucking legendary!" Nelson replied.

Peter chimed in with interest. "What's this?"

Allan and I remained silent listening to the story of Bart being charged with public drunkenness, then pulling out his bank card to pay the police officer.

Once they left the room I peered out the window and sighed, feeling the trip away was about to be ruined. I regret not leaving at this point when I had the opportunity and I'm sure I must have had a good reason at the time. I can't remember whether staying because of Peter, the difficulty getting home or fear of looking suspicious.

The next few days were a freckly version of cat and mouse. I'd wait for them to leave after hearing disturbing noises every time one of them came in to use the toilet, shower or kitchen. I would wake up and check the backyard making sure they were still asleep. I can still recall overhearing one of their conversations.

"Did you have sex last night?" Jimbo said.

"Nah I just played with some box," Bart replied, casually.

Peeping through a hole in the gate I looked for a box. Only later did I figure out what they were talking about. It was the first time I'd ever heard the word used in a sentence without meaning cardboard.

I remember wincing at Peter one night when we ordered pizzas for dinner. "Why are you including them?"

"Bart has offered to drive us to pick up," Peter replied.

Standing from the balcony, I watched him open the front passenger door waving me over. The driver window then opened and Bart's voice echoed down the street. "Travy! Get in the fucking car!"

Allan and I looked at each other. Neither of us wanted to go but at the time I thought avoiding him only made me look guilty.

My body sunk into the back seat as soon as I closed the door. Scrambling for the seatbelt, I looked over at Allan's white knuckles holding onto the door handle.

Thump! The house music erupted as the hairs inside my ears contracted. Peter laughed nervously as Bart smirked at me through his rear vision mirror, increasing the volume dial. Next to my foot I remember seeing a sealed bag of roughly twenty colored tablets.

Most were white but some had pinks and blues. At the time I assumed they were for nausea, but I look back now and realize what they really were. Bart had a keen eye for party drugs. Luckily, he never forced a party tab onto me and even luckier the three of us came away from Bart's reckless driving unscathed.

After returning home from the pickup Bart showered while we ate. It was difficult hearing the TV over the sound of his voice singing Metallica – Nothing Else Matters. Once finished, I still remember the bathroom door slowly creaking open and the light shining in my face. Bart spoke with a spine-chilling tone.

"Travy, I'm not wearing anything under this towel," he said.

I swallowed hard as the noise around me lifted. Bart stormed over and snatched the slice of pizza from my hand. Peter and Allan watched with horror when Bart took a large bite. I tried pushing him away, but it was no use. Using the force of gravity, he fell onto my lap, pinning me in between the table and my chair. I curled my toes, as the wet sensation from his towel absorbed into my shorts. Nelson and Jimbo laughed with pleasure when Bart got me in a headlock and pressed his lips against my forehead. Looking back now it was like a kiss of death. I quivered at the tingling sensation of a waterdrop running from his lips down my face. His lips then echoed dominating words into my ear.

"I'm going to fuck you bitch!" he said.

Finally, he hopped off and the abuse came to an end. It was just awful. I didn't feel like eating anymore pizza after that.

Even though it was obvious Bart was tormenting me he hadn't mentioned anything about the locker, which made me think either he no longer believed I was the culprit, or he no longer cared. Little did I know a tidal wave of chaos was coming towards me. At the time Bart's motives and intentions were unclear to me. The adult me however now sees the autism-induced false sense of reality which affected my judgement and decision making.

CHAPTER SEVENTEEN

PETER'S VOCAL CORDS frayed. "It wasn't me!"

I watched his face from afar turn from white to red.

"Is he fighting with Erika again?" I said.

Allan shrugged. I remember they had been having some issues before the trip after Peter made a crude comment about Erika's shoes. It didn't stop them regularly snapchatting each other, even during class. I remember working next to Peter while he typed away on his phone commenting on Erika's colorful outfit inside love heart frames.

"Check out her slutty boobs!" he'd say. I was never interested.

But he never shied away from talking to her in front of us, which made me question why he went outside. A few minutes later Peter came back in looking down at the carpet.

"That was dad," he said.

"Is he ok?" Allan replied.

He looked miserable. Whatever was said to him on the phone that day knocked him for six.

"Let's just go, I will fill you in later," Peter replied.

On our way to the pub Allan and I were doing most of the talking, which was unusual. We were usually the quiet ones around

Peter unable to get a word in. It wasn't until we walked down a narrow alleyway when Peter finally opened up.

"I have a meeting with the principal next week," he said.

I remember making a passing joke at him for being upset around returning his blazer, but his face remained grim. He then raised his voice in distress.

"I'm being accused of property damage!" he said.

I suddenly lost control on where I was walking and rolled my ankle on the edge of the gutter.

"What?" I said.

We all stopped, watching Peter's eyebrows droop down and together.

"I told him I know nothing about it, but I don't think he believes me," Peter said.

I massaged the ache in my foot. "Does this have anything to do with what I did?" I replied.

The moment Peter's eyes filled with tears, I felt sorry for him.

"Maybe," he replied.

At the time I couldn't see any other explanation. It had to be linked to the lockers and I was the only person in the year level aware of committing any property damage. The three of us were bamboozled on why Peter was now getting blamed for it. The topic dominated the chatter over dinner at the pub.

"Who told the principal?" Allan said.

Peter shook his head.

I remember we ran through all the possibilities on who it could be. Bart was immediately ruled out. Running to the principal simply wasn't his style and even if he did, he would've said something to us already, probably in his underwear!

Only Cameron and one other mate were involved with the original locker plans, and I couldn't picture any of them leaking lies to the principal. They'd be throwing themselves under the bus too.

I desperately wanted to know more but at this point we had

little information. All we knew was that someone had gone to the principal and accused Peter of property damage. The principal then had informed Peter's dad who clearly wasn't happy about it. And neither was Peter. Even in the lively atmosphere around us, he looked deflated. That night he didn't crack jokes or enjoy doing his usual impersonations with Allan. I remember grabbing his attention by kicking his shoe under the table.

"Any idea who it is?" I said.

"I know it wasn't you," he replied.

I laughed thinking why on earth I'd be such a fool. Ironically my adult self now believes I was in fact the fool sitting in the driver's seat with my foot on the accelerator.

Peter looked behind to check if anyone was listening in. It is here I still wonder now whether Peter had withheld any critical information and shared everything on his mind that night.

"It might be someone from down the road," he said.

I spilt my glass when he mentioned Cameron was staying with Scott and his friends only a few kilometers away. I half stood from my chair. "What! How do you know?" I said.

"Instagram," he replied.

Peter then showed a picture of about ten familiar faces from school fishing off the pier. Cameron was there at the back holding one of the rods. In that moment I realized Peter never fully explained why Cameron couldn't make it, and when I asked him the question his response was, "We only have five beds, and I couldn't say no to my cousin."

At the time I didn't understand what he was saying but later on found out he had never invited him at all. Peter had allowed Bart and his mates to sleep in the backyard but didn't invite Cameron to sleep inside the house. I remember feeling confused and thinking the whole thing was strange. I tried joining the dots many times but couldn't put anything together. Peter and Cameron didn't have any beef and even if they did, Cameron wouldn't be stupid enough to lie to the principal's face when he very well knew the truth.

Peter's cousin and his friend joined us at the pub later that night. Both never went to our school and had already celebrated their end of schooling last year. Given I'd never met them before and the emotional hype of the day's events I decided to leave and head back to the house. I simply needed time to myself to clear my thoughts and calm down. I wanted to be left alone in my own world. It's only now I realize this is a common emotional repair mechanism for autism, where the time in solitude helps to reduce the high levels of anxiety.

CHAPTER EIGHTEEN

HE STOOD OVER me on the balcony.

"You shit in Bart's locker!" Nelson said.

I had gone outside the house to collect my thongs when he randomly approached me from his tent. I remember ignoring him and looking down in search for the thongs when Jimbo came out and stood next to him in solidarity. "Yeah! You're on the cameras!" Even though my armpits were damp from fearful sweat I could tell from the smile on his face he was lying. Compared to the others, he didn't have the same level of hostility.

I hugged the railing as the party grew to four. This time a new face appeared; one I was dreading to avoid. Dirty Dolph, the long-haired scruff who served like a dog to Bart leaned forward and barked with aggression. Most of us at school believed he was the one involved with Miss Petrova because he dropped out shortly after the news became public. He was also seen as a womanizer, often walking around school with his arm wrapped over different girls. I remember one time out of nowhere he shoved me against a wall, then lifting me up he pressed his forearm into my neck, blocking off my airways. Luckily a teacher stopped him before it was too late. I also have a friend who still suffers trauma after he squirrel gripped his testicles in class. Reflecting on my past with him I think if things didn't turn out the way they did, Dolph was next in line to hear from vigilante Trav.

Feeling lightheaded, I crunched my toes into the ground waiting for their verbal punches to stop. The three of them kept going until I finally responded. I shrugged. "It wasn't me." A deep voice bellowed from inside the tent. He was listening to every word.

"Who was it then?" Bart said.

Dolph laughed at me. "Stop lying, we know it was you!" he said.

I remember thinking how do they know I'm lying? It must have been in my facial expressions or body language at the time. Like soldiers reporting to a military general, they all turned when Bart appeared clenching his fists. I stepped backwards and peered over the edge. They had cornered me between the balcony and the back door into the backyard. There was nowhere to go. I had to either jump over the railing and do a guilty runner or stay put and risk getting hammered. There was no happy ending to this. At the time I was frightened for my life.

"Why did you do it?" Dolph said.

Bart had positioned himself middle front, arms crossed, his eyes not leaving my face. I wish I had the courage to answer the question and verbalize the truth on what I thought of them. Bart took a step closer.

Jimbo chuckled. "Is it about the cock thing?" he said.

It was then I flashbacked to what happened back at school inside the room. That horrible day. Jimbo was there too, throwing Bart his trousers.

I didn't answer. Instead, I turned away giving myself a moment to calm my nerves. I felt sick. They kept pushing. I kept resisting. The words sat on the tip of my tongue, but I couldn't speak. There was only one way to make them stop. Closing my eyes I yelled over their voices.

"Alright! It was me, ok, I'm sorry!" I said.

Bart cheered, offering his mates a round of high fives. I opened my eyes. There was a small window of opportunity where I dashed like a greyhound, pivoting around Nelson and made it back inside.

Peter and Allan remained seated on the couch watching sports, oblivious to what was going on. At the time I was annoyed they hadn't stepped in but looking back I doubt there would've been any benefit. None of us had any fighting experience. Wasting no time, I collected my bags and bolted out the front door without saying goodbye. Just when I thought I had escaped a shadow shot out from the steps and blocked my tracks.

His voice was mean. "Where are you going?" he said.

My bags bounced off my shoulders. Bart repeated his question before I had the courage to respond.

"It was just a joke," I said. "The cock thing you did was a joke on me so I…"

Like a peacock spreading its feathers Bart widened his stance and raised his chest up to the sky. "How would you like it if I shit in your fucking face!"

The tension went up a notch as the other jocks made their way to the front of the house. I was caught in an ambush, and they'd blocked my exit. Sidestepping I reached for the wall, tripping over one of my bags.

It is here I say one of the strangest things ever. I don't know what was going on inside my head. At the time I was just desperate to get out of there and prepared to do anything.

"If I let you do that, would you forget the whole thing?" I said.

Bart raised his eyebrows, unsure how to respond then after a delay looked over his shoulder. Dolph shrugged and the others looked puzzled.

Bart turned back then hardened his lower lids. "Don't you think you deserve a punch in the face?"

My knees shook like I was standing in zero degrees.

"I've done kickboxing for the last five years, did you know that?" he said.

He cracked his knuckles as the others egged him on. Their faces were dripping with venom. My flight or fright response was in full swing however doomed to failure. I was powerless and clearly outnumbered.

I remember staring down at Bart's feet, apologizing profusely hoping they might let me go.

"Sorry for what I did to your locker," I said.

Bart roared in anger. "I don't care about that!" he replied.

I closed my eyes and squirmed, unsure by his response. Two of the jocks looked at one another with surprise.

"Huh?" Jimbo said.

I second guessed myself wondering if I was apologizing for the wrong thing. If Bart didn't care about what I'd done to his locker, then why had they hunted me down.

After a moment Bart provided an answer which still haunts me to this day. "You lied to me!"

My neck suddenly jolted sideways, once, then twice.

The jocks' shouted with praise. Numbness in my jawbone grew and I remember losing sensation in my face. The next few minutes are blurry, but I can recall stumbling down the road that day mesmerized by floating stars. Somehow, I made it to the station in one piece and hopped on the first train back home. It was the nadir of my high school life. I remember crying while rinsing the metallic taste of blood from my mouth. Luckily my jaw wasn't broken but they'd bruised it up pretty bad. I lied to my parents saying I had fallen over while drunk.

Back then the world around me was falling to pieces. Bart had punched me in the face because I'd lied to him when asked about vandalizing his locker. He didn't care about the damage to his items nor any disruption to his schooling. I wondered whether everyone else would react in a similar way. From this point it was only a matter of time before they found out. What would the school say? What would my parents say? I remember thinking they might tell me vandalism and revenge is ok as long as you don't lie about it when asked. I was extremely lost and confused because deep down the reasons for my actions still felt valid. But I didn't think anyone would understand. And I didn't fully understand it either. Why would anyone support someone who breaks into the school and drops his guts inside another student's locker?

It's only now I realize how alone I was, lost in my own world.

CHAPTER NINETEEN

MY PHONE ALERTED me with a text message. It was the one I had been waiting for.

"Hey mate, are you free now?" Peter said.

I ran down the road to his house on the other side of town. It had been ten days since returning from the trip and I was dying to find out how Peter's meeting went with the principal.

Peter's dad answered the door. I could tell from the look on his round face Peter had filled him in. I remember he laughed and pointed his finger.

"You've been a naughty boy!" he said.

We sat on the couch waiting for Peter to join us downstairs. Like many of the characters from the rugby club, Mr. Coobey was a big bodied alpha male. He also took pride in his BMW which I accidentally spoiled one time. Mr. Coobey was driving Peter and I to school and offered us chewing gum. I remember opening the electric window from the back seat and throwing mine away once it was finished. The next day I found out from two angry Coobeys my gum never made it outside the car and had shockingly lodged itself on the carpet flooring. Mr. Coobey then hired a detailer to have it dry-cleaned. I wasn't allowed anywhere near the car again. Mr. Coobey stretched his tree trunk arms.

"Pete, grab us a coke," he said.

We laughed when hearing Peter struggle getting the cans out from the fridge.

"Come on mate, it's just like pulling off a condom," he said.

He was a cheekier version of Peter and could always be relied on to share a crude joke. My family quickly became friendly with the Coobeys when they first moved into town. Mr. Coobey and dad got on like a house on fire, drinking beer, smoking and playing golf together on weekends. They were two Aussie blokes of similar age.

Peter sat on the couch slumped. "I'm being blamed for Scott's tablet," he said.

Mr. Coobey raised his eyebrows. "And you had nothing to do with it?"

Peter crossed his arms with frustration. "No!"

I looked around at the rugby memorabilia in their living room, waiting for their tiff to end. Even after Peter explained the situation multiple times, Mr. Coobey didn't seem totally convinced.

"I think I know who it is," Peter said.

I remember sliding to the end of my cushion, finding it difficult to keep still. At the time I really wanted to know who dobbed Peter into the principal.

"We had an argument before exams," he said.

"With Cameron?" I replied.

Peter shook his head. "Scott."

In that moment Peter's face changed. He then glanced at his dad from the corner of his eye. At the time I couldn't figure out why. Reading faces has never been one of my strengths, but afterwards found out Peter was keeping information from his dad. He had said as a result of family jealousy for the success of Plascom, Scott made up a story of seeing him use his PC tablet in class. He then went to the principal and accused him of stealing it. Back then I didn't ask any more questions and just accepted Peter's version of the events as the truth.

Mr. Coobey changed the seriousness of our conversation and chuckled. "I heard you covered up the cameras."

Peter and I joined the fun, making jokes on the ridiculous effort I had gone to.

"Look we know why you did it, I think it's funny, but we can't have Peter blamed for this," he said.

"We didn't tell the principal it was you," Peter said.

Mr. Coobey quickly chimed in. "But he knows you're covering for someone; have you told your folks?"

I shook my head as Peter and his dad crossed their legs in synchronization. Their posture and mannerisms on the chair were identical.

Mr. Coobey nodded. "It might be a good idea."

Our conversation that day ended under the agreement we would organize a meeting between the families after I told my parents. At the time I really didn't want to tell them anything but felt there was no other choice. If I refused, Peter would be in serious trouble and the friendship between Peter and our families would be over. Not to mention the ongoing internal family tensions, if my parents later on found out from the Coobey family.

Peter walked me out onto his verandah before shutting the door behind him. He lowered his voice into a half whisper. "Follow me."

He took me around to the garage which was linked to the side of his house. It had high ceilings with long beamed shelving, all of which were filled with plastering tins, tools and other random bits and bobs. I remember seeing an iconic Rabbitohs flag hanging in a window which I believe is still there at the time of writing this today.

I watched Peter reach deep into a black cupboard before handing me Scott's tablet.

"Take it," he said.

Again, I felt I had no choice. It was clear Peter wanted nothing to do with it and had wiped his hands clean of any evidence. Everything was on me.

I remember mulling over how I would even tell my parents. Do I tell them the whole story or leave out certain details? I didn't have the confidence or the knowledge to change the story like Peter did. When would I tell my parents? In the morning while eating my coco pops, at night over dinner or right before bedtime? How would they react? At the time I considered they might find it funny and laugh like Mr. Coobey. This could not be further from the truth. It turned into a long-winded, difficult and traumatizing conversation which stayed with me for years after. Even now as an adult I still don't know how people approach these types of decisions. Decisions which need consideration of the thoughts and feelings of other people.

There were a few days of procrastination before I finally broke the news to them.

"Mum, I need to tell you something," I said, facing her in the kitchen.

"Oh my god!" she said, after realizing Scott's tablet was hiding under the house. I had left it there whilst coming to a decision. The look of horror on her innocent face still haunts me to this day. I remember one time she stumbled upon the bolt cutters under my bed while cleaning my room. When she questioned me about it I had lied, saying they were borrowed from school to complete a project.

I remember telling dad about the events while he was working downstairs on his office computer. He was unable to focus and perform any work for the remainder of that day. Back then I felt confused because both my parents blamed themselves, questioning their parenting skills and trying to figure out where they went wrong. It was like they'd failed me, taking on ownership of my childish behavior and I had no idea why. I remember wanting to run away and start a new life somewhere else. I have great parents who only wanted the best for their children, always working hard and providing support whenever possible. It's only now as an adult I realize I had abused that privilege.

For months after the events at school I'd get questions from them on what I was doing and where I was going. Whenever needing to share big news such as getting a new job or buying a new car, mum's first response usually started with shock, "Oh no, what now!" It felt like she always expected the worst, preparing herself for what I might've done and what might come out of my mouth next. The sense of betrayal and lack of trust created a barrier between me and my parents which took years to repair.

CHAPTER TWENTY

"G'DAY MATE, DO you want a beer?" Dad said.

I remember laughing, hearing him from inside my bedroom. I'm sure the last thing Mr. Coobey wanted that night was a beer to celebrate his son being accused of property damage. Dad greeted Peter and his parents the same way he welcomed anyone else into our house. Like it was a party. Regardless of who the person was or why they were visiting, he never failed to greet them with excitement then offer an alcoholic drink or coffee. And if refused, he would keep asking them "are you sure?" until the person finally caved in from the guilt of saying no. He even offered second drinks well before people finished their first. It was one of his many likeable qualities. With his Steve Irwin like charisma most described dad as a man who's never had a bad day in his life. One of my high school friends even said to me one time, "Why can't you be more like your dad?".

My mum on the other hand was the polar opposite. Quiet, caring and risk-averse she kept our family in order, constantly thinking in advance and planning ahead for family birthday and Christmas celebrations. Without her nothing would've ever got done.

After exchanging pleasantries, our parents got down to business. I sat in silence at the end of the dining table letting the grown-ups do all the talking.

"Put your phone away!" Mr. Coobey said.

Peter jumped. Even though he had an addiction I couldn't blame him. I would've rather been on my phone that night too.

After some of the mischievous details were revealed, I remember Peter's mum pulled a surprised face, "You boys are worse than the girls."

Dad stood from his chair and shared a story of how he dealt with bullies when he was at school. "Back in my day you'd punch them in the nose and that was the end of it."

Even if I had the courage to throw punches, I honestly can't imagine Scott or Bart ever backing down in that situation. It would end very badly.

Mr. Coobey joined in with more tough guy stories. "That's exactly how we did it on the field," he said.

He then spoke of his rugby coaching days on how all the boys in the team looked out for each other. Like a wolfpack if one of them was attacked or in a fight the others would immediately step in for support. Strangely enough Peter has never given off the same vibe so maybe it's a generation thing. Overall, the Coobeys didn't appear upset that night but rather entertained by what I'd done. I remember feeling relieved hoping it might take some pressure off me however my parents' disapproval remained rock solid.

"We know why you did it, we think it's funny, but we can't have this under Peter's name, he's the school captain!" Mr. Coobey said.

My parents turned to one another before nodding in agreeance. Looking back now I believe the intentions of the Coobey family were clear. I simply needed to come forward and clear Peter's name to save his reputation. Even though I didn't really have a choice, it felt like the right thing to do. My parents had also sided with the Coobeys, so I was largely outnumbered. It felt like I was both a rogue and a savior, someone who can wave their magic wand and erase all the problems, yet at the same time be the one responsible for creating them. I often wondered over the years how Peter and his parents would have handled the situation if he wasn't the school captain. Would they still be asking me to clear his name? Would it still be as big of a problem? At the end of the day my confession of the truth and helping erase the allegations against Peter was the most morally correct thing I ever did. One of the few positive outcomes and proudest moments from the high school saga.

I remember walking into the principal's office wearing out the soles of my shoes. After finishing exams, I never wanted any reason to return to the school.

Both mum and dad were there sitting beside me around a white circular table. I remember mum was very quiet looking worried and dad sat with his arms crossed giving the impression he didn't want to be there. Mum had dragged him along. He even snapped at the vice-principal when she came in to offer us tea and coffee.

"That sheila is a dickhead!" he said.

Dad always considered himself a good judge of character but looking back now I don't know how he could've summed up the vice-principal from a 10 second conversation. However, I've come to learn most people can draw conclusions and form opinions on people within the first seven seconds of a first impression. I don't believe I've ever achieved this timeframe and it's rare I reach a judgement on anyone. Unless it's obvious the person might be trouble (for example Bart) it's just not something I ever think about. There are too many variables.

Principal Sheffield came in and joined us at the circular table. He wore his regular custom-made suit which made him look more like a banker than a principal. At the time he was relatively new to Egan High having transferred across from a prestige Private school. I remember on his first day we were all required to stand and show him respect when he entered the room for an introduction.

"Thank you for coming in today, I believe you have some information regarding the theft from Scott Read's locker?" The principal said.

Slouching my shoulders down, I sighed. Dad nudged me with his elbow. "Go on tell him."

Feeling extremely uncomfortable I said, "It wasn't Peter, it was me." The principal leaned forward with interest.

At this point I remember weeping struggling to continue. "The things Scott says, it's been going on for years, it felt good to finally get back at him."

The principal wrote down notes as I described the day at the stairs when Scott broke my calculator and shared examples of his verbal abuse. There were many pauses because I found it extremely difficult to talk. I jumbled up words and chose the wrong word for the sentence, making me worry no one would believe what I was saying.

"I also did something bad to Bart Osbourne's locker," I said.

The principal looked uncomfortable priming his collar.

"Don't you worry about him, we understand why," he replied.

I look back on this moment now and think how strange it was for the principal to justify my actions against Bart but not Scott. Even though it was a win not having to talk about the Bart related issues, overall the school handled things poorly. Our meeting focused only on Scott's tablet and anything to do with Bart was brushed aside. At the time I assumed he already had enough on his plate with Bart. I remember hearing he was being investigated by police under the grounds of acting as an accomplice in the teacher-student relationship. The drama with Miss Petrova had spiraled out of control and was seriously tarnishing the school's reputation.

To quantify things more there were 150 students who graduated in my year level and only 36 new enrolments the following year. To be honest I'm surprised the government never shut it down. It took another eight years under a new principal and management team to return it back to normal levels. Ironically today Egan High is ranked in the top 10 best government schools in the state. I certainly missed out and jealously wish I could go back and finish my high school education again!

The principal turned to my parents.

"Look we understand as parents you may feel responsible for his behavior," he said.

I remember peeping through my fingers, watching mum cry. Of everyone around the table listening to my version of events she appeared the most hurt. The principal stood from his chair and spoke elegantly.

"Generally something of this nature, would definitely result in a suspension, if not expulsion, however given the year has now finished, all we can really do is prohibit Travis attending his graduation ceremony. We trust as parents you'll have your own form of punishment," he said.

"Shit yeah!" Dad replied.

The principal looked spooked by his response. For better or worse dad always found a way of changing the tempo in a conversation.

Before leaving I was asked one last question which I remember being the most difficult to answer.

"Who else did you tell?" he said.

Like a guilty man, I pulled my hair, desperate to focus on something else. I held my breath from the word bullets fired into my chest. The vice-principal froze mid-air with her pen waiting for my response.

He spoke firmly. "We need to know."

I watched the principal's eyes light up with anticipation. I looked up at the low ceiling, pretending to think. The time window had passed and whatever my response was that day would've appeared incompetent.

I strained. "Peter Coobey and Allan Buckley," I replied.

The principal lifted his pointy chin. "No one else?"

I could've added another three people but chose to stay silent and shake my head. Back then I figured Cameron was somehow involved in the allegations, so I decided not to throw him under the bus. Only months after when the dust settled did I discover that Cameron had nothing to do with it and had impressively kept the secret to himself the entire time. I wanted to protect as many friends as possible. Who knows what might've happened if the wrong people found out they were involved with my theft and vandalism of school property. All my mates had put their lives on the line and without their help I wouldn't have been able to pull it off.

Over the following days Peter and Allan were called into the school to verify my story to the principal. As expected, only Peter showed up. Allan didn't even pick up the phone.

For as long as we've known Allan he has been unreliable, living the life of a recluse. Rarely does he answer his phone or respond to a simple message. As mentioned earlier none of us believe he's ever committed to a regular job, anyone or anything. Although never diagnosed, it wouldn't surprise me if he was also on the autism spectrum.

CHAPTER TWENTY-ONE

I STEPPED BACK from the dining table. "Do I have to go? I said.

Mum slammed her hand on the bench. "Yes! You're apologizing to Scott!"

I still remember the fury in her eyes. She was deeply troubled, not just by what I did but the way she had found out. I look back now and believe the lying and deceit behind my crimes caused more damage than the crimes themselves.

I tucked in, hiding behind her when she knocked on the Read family front door. I remember all four of them stood side by side, grimacing. I had no idea what they were about to say or do. Confessing to my parents and the principal was hard enough, but standing face to face with Scott and his family inside their house was petrifying. The whole family were affected in some way by my actions. If it wasn't for the pleasant smell of warm baked bread I would've turned around and ran away. Thinking about it now perhaps Scott was right about one thing. He often announced his mum was the best cook in the world.

Without looking at anyone's face I placed Scott's tablet down on a bench.

"We're here to return your tablet and apologize," I said.

Scott's voice flared into escalation. "What's the significance of the condom?"

Mum closed her eyes as her body stiffened. I had completely forgotten about the condom. On the day of stealing his tablet I left behind a condom filled with red dye inside his locker. Unused of course! The idea came to me after overhearing the conversation between Scott and the jocks. The one where someone bled from pulling himself too hard. My thought was to leave behind a clue in the hope Scott would be misled to believe the culprit was one of the jocks. My mates loved the idea. Of all the things to talk about, I didn't expect his first question to be about the condom. Unfortunately, it turned out to be the most damaging part, which I now deeply regret.

I stuttered filler sounds not knowing how to respond.

Scott grinded his teeth while I tried to downplay the condom prank.

"It's from The Simpsons," I said.

He didn't flinch. His mum raised one eyebrow at me. After an awkward silence I remember Scott responded with rage.

"I was in hospital this year with a ruptured kidney," he said.

My eyes jumped from their sockets. It turned out earlier in the year, Scott had spent time in hospital with kidney problems which caused him to urinate blood. Afterwards I joined the dots and realized Scott believed the condom with red dye was a sickening attempt to mock him. If it wasn't for the adults in the room, he would've torn me to shreds that day. The prank had him totally baffled because he said the only person who knew about his kidney issues was his girlfriend.

"When I found out you were involved, I took it out on your brother at cricket training, bowling at his head," Scott said. Watching him signal hand gestures, I pulled my shirt over my face. My brother Jack and him happened to play at the same local club in Flat

Rock. Interestingly Jack has no memory of Scott at cricket training bowling at his head.

"I felt like I was on a cliff, leaning over the edge. Why did you do it?" Scott said.

I remember holding myself back from crying as he raised his voice.

"You've been harassing me, saying things for years," I replied.

Before I had a chance to mention the calculator incident, he cut me off.

"I didn't think you actually cared," Scott said.

I thought to myself, how can someone who dishes out so much verbal abuse believe no one would care. It's only now I understand the years of failing to speak up and pretending to ignore Scott led him to think he could do whatever he pleased. I should've stood up for myself early on when I had a chance but back then I didn't know how.

When I explained there were others he upset and others who supported my actions he cut me off again.

"I went through every person in the year level and never thought you would do it, I still don't," Scott said.

The hairs on my arms and ears pricked up. I remember freezing as our conversation with the Read family suddenly took a nasty turn.

"I want to know how much Peter was involved, even if it was like 0.001 percent," Scott said.

I nervously pulled the rough fabric of my shirt, shocked by his response.

"It wasn't Peter, it was me!" I replied.

Mrs. Read finally joined in. Prior to going over I had expected her to do most of the talking but for some reason that day she remained silent.

"Don't feel you have to come here and cover for him, we know he's the real culprit," she said.

I looked across at Scott's father shaking his head.

"We've had enough," he said.

Mrs. Read's face turned red as she went on one of her long rants about the letters she'd wrote to the school, threatening to remove her kids if the situation wasn't dealt with. Scott's younger brother also broke his silence.

"I fucking hate Egan High. I'm leaving at the end of the year."

Mrs. Read squeezed his arm after he cursed then expressed her distaste for the Coobey family.

"Egan High is sweeping this under the carpet to protect the loveable school captain." I remember her saying the word "loveable" with a different tone which I've come to realize was her sarcasm.

"Peter sat next to me in class, using my tablet," Scott said.

At the time I believed him but looking back at this now I don't believe Peter would've been so foolish. Mum had dragged me to the Reads' house that day to return Scott's tablet and apologize but our conversation somehow ended into a rambling nonsense about Peter. It was like I had to prove to them I was behind it all. I remember leaving thinking we should've simply left the tablet on their doormat with a smiley face note. It reached the point where mum and I couldn't bear to listen to any more badmouthing of Peter. Mum nudged me forward.

"Look, I'm sorry," I said.

Staring at the floor I offered a handshake. Scott looked up at his parents who gave a nod of approval. He then reached out and squeezed my hand so tight my fingers went numb. I left shortly after and waited in the car while mum stayed back and spoke with Mrs. Read. She asked to speak to her in private. I remember on our way back home; mum shook her head in frustration.

"So did you actually do this or was it Peter?" she said.

I got agitated. "It was me! Peter knew about it, that's it."

Her curly hair sunk into the headrest as she planted the accelerator. "You better not be lying again!"

I sat in the back seat, staring out the window wondering how on earth things ended up in such a mess. And to make things even worse Mrs. Read asked my mum for compensation to cover the cost of Scott's replacement tablet. Apparently over the past few months Scott had been using another tablet which his parents had gone out and purchased. By the time I explained the full story on how Scott destroyed my calculator she had already paid Mrs. Read the money. I'm not sure whether it was the way I explained myself or the lack of trust, but she never totally believed my version of the events. This made things so hard. Back then it felt no one was on my side.

A few weeks later my savings account took a $325 blow. Part of my punishment was to pay for the compensation. A lot of money for an 18-year-old. Luckily though I was a good saver. A few weeks earlier I'd bought my first car without any parental support. One thing I can thank my autism for are my savvy financial skills. I've always been strong in maths, hence why I was selected for the advanced maths class. I think it's because numbers never lie. They're always fixed and never have any underlying feelings or emotions like so many other opaque things in life. I'm not surprised many of us on the spectrum find ourselves in accounting and finance-related careers.

CHAPTER TWENTY-TWO

I HAVE NO regrets missing my graduation ceremony. If anything, it was a blessing not having to face Scott or Bart. The school posted my certificates to the house which are currently still framed, hanging inside my bedroom.

Shortly after everything unfolded there were confrontations between the Coobey and Read families. I heard about some of the heated phone calls where both families blamed one another over the tablet I had stolen. There was also some argy-bargy on the field one time during a rugby match when Scott's team were playing another team coached by Mr. Coobey. He had ordered some of his larger players to target Scott and take him out of the game.

To this day I still don't understand why they had a falling out after I clearly confessed to the crime and apologized. It was never my intention to cause fighting between families. I simply only wanted to get even with Scott for his ongoing harassment and breaking my calculator.

Even after being punished, the remnants of high school lingered, particularly when attending 18th birthdays the following year. I remember having a conversation with Cameron.

"Did you invite Scott to your birthday?" I said.

He replied with sincerity. "Yeah, sorry mate."

I sat inside my car for fifteen minutes contemplating whether to go inside his house. I didn't think Scott would show up and even if he did, I thought he would've moved on. Roughly six months had passed since the day I returned his tablet. But on the night, within seconds of greeting friends and shaking hands, an angry boy from our year broke through my comfort zone. His eyebrows furrowed.

"Why the fuck are you showing your face around here!" he said.

I stepped back from his aggression, but he clearly wasn't backing down. He wanted a piece of me as they say. It felt like I was pulling his chest with a lasso. He then shoved my body towards the wall.

"It had nothing to do with you!" I said.

Luckily someone stepped in and pulled him away. I remember the New York hat he wore fell off his head and crashed onto the ground.

"You little prick, why would you do that!" he said.

A shiver went down my spine when Scott patted his back and smiled. I didn't know those two were friends. I also didn't know how many others at the party shared the same feelings. Given how uncomfortable the night was I left shortly after the incident. Only now do I understand the reason why Peter never showed to many high school birthdays. Interestingly I ran into this friend of Scott years later and when I brought up this encounter from the party, he had no memory of it.

"I've taken a lot of drugs since then," was his reply.

That was the last time I ever saw Scott. For years I felt deep regret for the trauma and feuding I'd caused him and his family. Especially when finding out about his bladder infection. Although I was furious when he broke my calculator, in my eyes what I did to him was very wrong and inappropriate. I also didn't like the way things ended between us which left a yearning of unfinished business to reconnect with him again in the future.

I can't say I shared this same yearning towards Bart. After what happened at Peter's beach house, I never wanted to see him again. However I've come to learn sometimes life throws grenades at you which can feel impossible to dodge. Sure enough two years later Bart showed up at Jack's presentation awards night. At the time Jack happened to be school captain so we all went along to support. I didn't know why Bart was there but found out later on he'd bought a ticket to flirt with one of the girl performers. I kept my distance from his movements the whole night. From my table I watched him place his hands over my sister's hips on the dancefloor. Standing up from my seat, he pulled her towards his privates, then staring at me stuck out his tongue while grinding against her backside. Of the four hundred guests (including my sister) I was the only one sober enough to notice.

I remember feeling my blood vessels dilate. Like an animal in the wild I wanted to attack but looking around at family and friends having fun, I sat down waiting for him to leave. The night still remains in my long-term memory, in fact many things from high school still do. Often neurodivergent individuals have a superior long-term memory, which makes it extremely difficult to forget things which are better off forgotten. For this reason, we are more vulnerable to the long-term impacts of trauma and PTSD.

When I was younger, I felt proud on what I did to Bart and regretted not taking things further when I had the chance. In my opinion what he'd done to me outweighed anything I did in return so overall I was the loser. He has never apologized or showed any remorse for his actions. For years his face haunted me, and flashbacks from high school would trigger bad memories and crush my self-esteem. I believe this in turn hindered my social development and ability to maintain relationships because it took a long time before I could trust anyone. Romantic relationships were non-existent until well after finishing high school.

I'm no murderer but admit to having thoughts of doing bad things to Bart, settling the score. My psychologist has referred to these feelings as autistic malice i.e. Whatever you do to me, I can do to you. I don't like these thoughts and it took years to build enough strength to forgive him for what he did and move forward. I never had this strength in high school but believe writing this story has helped come to terms with it and allowed me to reach closure. Last I heard Bart has moved abroad, so I hope wherever in the world he is today, he's matured into a responsible adult.

As touched on already the most rewarding part of the high school saga was coming forward to clear Peter's name. This has made an everlasting impression on our friendship he has never forgotten. "I know why you did it, it has brought us closer together," he has said.

To this day we are still close mates and often joke about what happened in the company of friends. However the jokes are centered around my immaturities, and less around him or anyone else's involvement.

One fact I still haven't totally come to terms with was how information leaked out to the principal and why Peter was being held accountable. I've never believed Peter actually sat next to Scott in class and pulled out his tablet in front of him. It is more likely someone has spilt the beans and teamed up with Scott for him to go to the principal and blame Peter. For a long time I assumed it was Cameron, however it wasn't until about a year after graduating when Peter was asked about Erika.

"Hate that slimy bitch!" he said.

"Was she the one who told Scott?" I said.

I remember we were out drinking at a university bar, and I desperately wanted to know. I've always had a burning desire to seek knowledge and find out why things happen. And whenever someone puts a roadblock up in front of me, I get very irritated. This is a classic symptom of ADHD. Patience is extremely difficult. Other difficulties include waiting in lines, getting stuck in peak hour traffic and holding on when needing to use the toilet. As the story continues, you'll see how this has caused me grief.

Peter's face turned bright red before he answered defensively, "No, it was Scott!"

There was a possibility Erika was somehow involved since she was the principal's niece and wasn't exactly the sharpest tool in the shed.

"Did you tell Erika about the lockers?" I said.

We poked him a few times that night however he never opened up. He still hasn't. I've tried several times and Peter continually declines, making it abundantly clear to protect his mental health, he can't discuss any negative experiences, past or present. I became annoyed and bitter with him over this, especially after I'd confessed to clear his name. It's taken me a long time to let it go and respect Peter's wishes. To this day whenever we bring up either Erika or Scott and his family the conversation turns awkward. Whatever happened back then will remain an unsolved mystery.

It would be nice to know how everything unraveled. After all I was punched twice in the face, refused entry to my high school graduation and forced to confront Scott's family and pay them from my savings account. If not for that person or persons, I would've likely got away with everything. But perhaps I have someone to thank?

From the eyes of a wiser adult looking back I believe I deserved to be caught and punished for my crimes. Who knows what future trouble may have evolved had I never been caught. It's shaped me into becoming a better person. If there's one thing I know now, it's undisciplined bad behavior only promotes more bad behavior.

ACT 2
UNIVERSITY AND EARLY-CAREER

CHAPTER TWENTY-THREE

AFTER LEAVING EGAN High to study Science at University, I started to transform. It was like my life was reset and the burden of high school quickly faded. The new environment allowed me to meet new people and make new friends boosting my confidence and self-esteem. Improvements in my persona were noticed not only by my parents but also previous high schoolers who saw me over the following years. I remember walking around the university campus alongside attractive female faces with a smile on my face. None of them knew of my past history and assumed I was one of the cool kids. I began talking to girls, some of which I spent time with on weekends attending parties and nightclubs in the city. I was always the designated driver, making sure friends got home safe at the end of a late night. However for reasons I couldn't explain in the midst of the transformation, unexpected learning and behavioral problems continued to emerge.

During my final year, I completed a 3000-word literature review for a compulsory subject, which was needed to graduate for the degree. The project involved research of a chosen topic, reading and comprehending lots of journal articles, citing and referencing before submitting into a plagiarism software program. The program calculated how much the writing related back to other published work. To pass everyone needed to achieve a score lower than 10%.

My first submission was 56%.

My second submission was 42%.

My third submission was 25%.

"We can't pass you with this review!" the subject coordinator said.

I raised my voice in frustration at the lady, "But I didn't plagiarize!" Standing up from my chair I explained how hard I'd worked on the project, staying up late at night. I remember showing her copies of all the journal articles printed out and scattered across my desk. She shook her head in dismay and failed me.

Failing the subject meant I had to re-enroll and repeat the following year otherwise I wasn't graduating. It also meant paying a second set of education fees.

I got angry because it didn't make any sense. All my friends cruised through the subject, passing with little effort, even the ones I knew I was smarter than. Everyone I spoke with achieved plagiarism scores of less than 10%, if not on their first submission definitely by their second. What went wrong? And why was it so hard for me? At the time I assumed either there was a computer glitch, or I needed to work harder. Little did I know what was actually holding me back. The inside of my brain!

Unable to swallow the pill I decided to write a formal letter and appeal my academic record with the Faculty of Science. After begging them to reconsider they gave me one more chance to submit another literature review. Luckily this time my plagiarism result scraped in at 9%. I jumped for the sky when my Fail changed to a Pass.

CHAPTER TWENTY-FOUR

I'LL NEVER FORGET one person who found the subject easy. She was studying a double degree in law and science and happened to fall into one of my classes. Tall with dark African skin, she had a coy smile of invitation which I didn't know how to read.

She sat next to me one day in a lecture and the scent of her sandalwood perfume stole my attention.

"Hey! Have you got a ruler?" she said.

I was then introduced to her a few weeks later through a mutual friend, which was when she finally returned my ruler. Once we were paired up on a group project our friendship bloomed. But others around campus who noticed us walking around together expressed concerns. One time I was even pulled outside.

"Stay away from Imani!" Two girls said to me.

"Huh?" I replied.

I saw the fear in their eyes but didn't understand why they were warning me. At the time I thought there was no chance I'd score with her. Not only was she out of my league, but she was dating someone else at the time. Imani was one of those girls who always seemed to be taken. She'd previously broken up with a long-term boyfriend and within a few weeks had already found someone else.

One of the girls poked me in the arm. "You can do so much better, we'll find you a nice girl."

I scratched my head and remembered thinking, how can they tell she wasn't nice? I never heard her yell verbal abuse, watch her ram people into walls, stick wet fingers into people's ears or threaten to punch anyone in the face. She even apologized when forgetting to return my ruler. Back then my only gauge of who was nice and who wasn't was by comparing them to Scott and Bart. Every time I saw Imani around campus she smiled and waved to say hi with a friendly face. Aside from the bizarre rumor floating around, she was a prize.

All the warnings went in one ear and out the other and I quickly forgot the advice I was given. Imani and I became closer.

"Why do you keep touching my knee?" I said.

A shiver ran down my spine. It was the same knee Bart had grabbed three years earlier. She giggled, showing no interest in her computer screen. She had followed me to the library to work on a case study but looking back now it was more like the introduction of a porno.

I remember her gentle touch over my pants sparked a tingling sensation down my neck. I tried to focus on completing the work but couldn't concentrate without getting side-tracked. A common symptom of autism is a hypersensitivity to being touched, especially when sudden or unexpected.

"What do you like in girls?" she said.

I kept staring at the screen all hot in the face unsure how to respond. She then leant over my shoulder and whispered into my ear with a pleasurable tone. "How many have you been with?"

How do you know if someone is flirting, joking around or just being overly friendly? The answer is never clearcut. Most teenagers develop this skill over their high school years from the trial and errors of experimenting with others. At the age of 21 I was sitting next to a beautiful girl in the library who was projecting herself onto me and I had no idea what to do.

I remember a boy watching us from across his desk winked at me with a grin and moved his lips in silence. Lip reading has never been one of my strengths but managed to make out his repeated words, "You're in."

A few minutes passed before I shut my computer down and decided to leave but for some reason Imani wanted me to stay.

She tugged my shirt, "Come with me," she said.

As we headed upstairs, my curiosity got the better of me.

"Am I in?" I said.

She looked at me and squinted. "Huh?"

I was too afraid to repeat the question. She took me up to the top floor and down to the very end corner of the building. We passed several aisles of bookshelves. I'd never been to this area of the library before. It only had bare walls and a door which was signed, "staff access only".

I watched Imani open it with ease. It was like she'd done it many times before. "Go in," she said.

I remember hesitating and looking around. She laughed. "Just go in!"

The room was tiny with only a few shelves holding books and some boxes with lost property. It looked uninhabited and smelt like dust. Sitting down on the only chair I knew something was about to happen but didn't know what.

"Where are we?" I said.

My palms felt sweaty with anxious thoughts of whether I was about to be locked inside, kidnapped, molested or murdered. Imani shut the door and removed her top. She was wearing a black bra with sheer lace. My jaw dropped. She exhaled. She pushed my shoulders back into the chair and sat on top of my knees. With one long leg stretching either side of my torso she leant in to kiss my lips. I remember a wave of fear consumed me and I ducked my head, blocking her with my arms.

"I don't want to get you sick," I said.

Back then I was recovering from symptoms of glandular fever which is a contagious virus transmitted through saliva. I remember I calculated the incubation time (the time between exposure and onset of symptoms) and was able to trace back to the person I'd caught it from. And when I reached out to let this girl know she was infectious, she called me a prick.

When I warned Imani about my glandular fever, I was surprised it didn't faze her.

She pulled my arms down with arousing force, "I don't care!"

I remember hearing her aggressive consent opened the floodgates to a new world I'd never been before. Her red lips pressing into my neck sparked powerful energies, erecting hair and reflexes causing goosebumps over my skin. Any leftover fatigue from the virus had dissipated and all my worries seemed to disappear. It was like whatever was happening in the world around us no longer mattered. Imani was in a trance and had taken me along for the ride. She raised my arms and pulled off my shirt with delight.

"You're so white," she said.

She ran her colorful fingernails over my nipples. The same ones Scott reached for years ago, only this time was different. This time I wanted it. I remember the blood-rush feeling, like electric fireworks erupting throughout different parts of my body. It was liberating. I felt alive. Up until that point I'd never had a girl show interest in me, at least none I knew about.

My only experience of romance was from watching movies. I remember just as things were heating up in the library that day Jim Levenstein from American Pie came to mind. Suddenly his character consumed my head and I said something incredibly foolish.

"You smell like my sister," I said.

Imani dropped my shirt on the floor, "Ok, that's just weird." I shut my eyes and dropped my chin, then mumbled words, trying to think of something rhyming with sister. She raised her eyebrows.

"Perfume! You smell like perfume," I said.

She smiled fondly. Although I'd completely ruined the moment, somehow just like Jim had done with Nadia inside his bedroom, I'd made a grand recovery. The fun continued. She pushed her chest so close into mine I could count her heartbeats. Twisting, turning, touching she knew what she was doing. I remember my head throbbing and watching a small mirror next to us fog up as things got hot and steamy. Then it happened. Before I had a chance to stare down third base the exciting intimacy came to a halt.

Imani cringed, "You're bleeding!" she said.

I opened my eyes in horror at the sight of blood caked around her lips and cheeks.

"No, you're bleeding!" I replied.

It turns out guys can have periods too. My nose had been bleeding away in the background unnoticed. I have a long history of blood noses, but never did they happen without blowing hard into a tissue. Looking back it must have been the overheating excitement from the intimacy causing me to blow a fuse. The opportunity to lose my virginity inside the university library that day was postponed. As I write about it now it sounds disappointing but at the time I remember feeling on top of the world ready to take on the next challenge with Imani.

When I was told she had tarnished friendships for being a compulsive liar it didn't faze me. I couldn't tell when she was lying or telling the truth anyway. According to the rumors at the time she was being investigated by police after being caught on camera stealing makeup and skin care products from a David Jones. Apparently she denied all the charges and said it was her cousin with a similar appearance.

It puzzled me why she'd shoplift from a store and forget to cover up the cameras. That's just amateur!

"Don't believe them, it's not true. Our family is fighting over money," she said.

The stories didn't quite add up so I didn't believe she would do such a silly thing, and even if she did, it didn't change my growing attraction towards her. She'd opened the door to a mix of new experiences. Things I'd never considered before were circulating in my head and I wanted to learn more. She was very attractive, so at the time it made sense because she liked me, I had to like her back. I thought it was love, but over the coming weeks I discovered it was far from it.

CHAPTER TWENTY-FIVE

I STILL REMEMBER the day she strutted towards me in the university cafeteria. "He doesn't want me to talk to you," she said.

I squinted with bewilderment. "I thought you said you two were over?" I replied.

Imani curled her upper lip, "No, that was my ex."

I scratched my head, second guessing my understanding of the word "ex".

She walked off in a huff while I took a second to join the dots. "She must be lying again" I thought. Since the day in the library, we had spoken every day, either in person or online and just 12 hours earlier we'd spoke on the phone for over an hour. She had also made the trip out to my house and had dinner with me and my parents. Where would she find the time to date someone else? And why would a guy I'd never met tell me to stop talking to someone? I remember playing it over in my head unable to figure it out. Then the next day we saw each other and worked in class like nothing ever happened. It was weird. None of it made sense so at the time I didn't know how to feel. Maybe this is what relationships are really like I thought.

But things got weirder. I'll never forget the night I fell out of my computer chair, in shock by the message on the screen:

Rohan_lookin2tuff wants to talk with you on messenger.

Immediately I messaged Imani, "Did you tell Rohan my email?"

"Huh? No, why's that?" she replied.

Without a second thought I naively accepted the request, thinking it must be someone else.

"Hey bro stay the fuck away from Imani,"
"I know you're still talking to her,"
"Tomorrow at uni I will stab you."

My jaw dropped. Gripping onto the armrests I felt like I was inside an airplane, flying through turbulence. Reading his words over I could feel the blood boiling under my skin. "Why does this guy want to hurt me? I thought.

I stared at the screen rubbing the back of my neck for ten minutes. What do you say to someone when they threaten you? Reflecting back on high school times with Scott and Bart I wrote down a collection of different ways to respond:

What time?
It wasn't me!
Are you joking?
Be right back.
If I let you do that, would you forget the whole thing?

After careful consideration I typed the words "Be right back" hoping he'd think I was too busy to read his message. Of course I laugh at this now. Facebook messenger can tell you when someone has read your message.

Tossing and turning in bed I contemplated whether to show up to my 9am lecture. I was scared for my life. From what Imani had told me, Rohan was the jealous boyfriend type with a hot temper. He had previously beaten a guy up after he flirted with her one time. Jealousy is something I've never understood. I believe it to be the most irrational and incorrect feeling people have. Unless the person has a more successful and high achieving identical twin out there it's complete nonsense worrying about other people.

Rohan dropped out of school and worked on cars in a garage on the other side of the city which made me think why would he skip work and drive an hour out of his way to chase me around a university? Once again, my predictions were wrong.

Entering the lecture theatre, my heart skipped a beat. Someone giggled. Straight away I knew who it was. My knees trembled watching a tattooed arm in the front row, wrap around her neck. The same neck which was splattered with my blood a few weeks earlier. I scanned the audience for a seat pretending not to see them.

"Hey Trav!" someone said.

I bit my tongue forcing myself to ignore the mate wanting my attention. They both turned. Our eyes made contact. I stared blankly into the space between everyone, calculating my next move. My mate looked down at Imani in front of him and realized his mistake. I remember thinking, "Speak now or forever hold your peace".

I didn't know what to say so I raised my arm and pointed, then scrunching up my face like Uncle Sam, I marched forward. Imani pinched his shoulder stopping Rohan from getting up. You could tell from his torn outfit he wasn't here to learn about the neurosensory pathways of the spinal cord. As I got closer his thin eyebrows dropped and his boney cheeks tensed with grit. "He's totally surrounded, only a fool would pull out a knife" I thought.

I took a deep breath, cleared my throat then said with a school principal tone, "I want to speak to both of you after this lecture."

Imani and Rohan looked at each other. I vanished up the stairs before they had a chance to respond, but on my way heard the faint words from a familiar female voice, "don't."

Sitting in the back row, my eyes never left them. I remember being unable to listen to the lecturer because my mind drifted into another dimension, hyper focusing on what was locking me inside a fight-or-flight response.

After the lecture I watched them abruptly exit the theatre and believed I'd scared them away. But before I could sigh with relief my toes suddenly pressed into the floor. My body felt like I was in the passenger seat next to my dad behind the wheel. He jerks and slams on the brakes at intersections before yelling "dickhead" at other drivers. I've had to take his demerit points at times to stop the law taking away his license.

Imani stood with her back to me in the foyer, her hand reaching for her man walking off in the other direction. It was then I knew Rohan wasn't going to stab me. Standing tall with watery eyes I felt a tidal wave of emotions consume me. None of which I can properly describe.

My voice wounded with hurt. "Do you know what he said to me?" I said.

She shrugged. I then explained how much she's damaged everything between us.

"We were never in a relationship," she replied.

"Yes, we were! You've lied to everyone and lost all your friends and now you've lost me!" I said.

She tried to say something rude, but I cut her off. "Both of you just fuck off and get out of my life!"

I remember looking down into the sweaty palms of my hands wondering what had come over me. It was the first time in my life anger had tipped me over the edge and I was able to voice it to someone with words and gestures. Up until this point I'd suppressed negative feelings, run away and hidden from confrontation in order to plot an evil plan of revenge. Not on this occasion!

It felt incredibly good to release some energy, however I still ended up in the dumps with a broken heart. My friends who warned me from the beginning could see the writing on the wall, and I didn't listen. At the time I was rattled by the way things ended and it was some time before I found the courage to date someone else. It's only now I realize how much I was blindsided by my undiagnosed conditions, pursuing Imani without considering the harmful consequences.

CHAPTER TWENTY-SIX

WITH THE EXCEPTION of avoiding the career path of Imani, I wasn't sure what I wanted to do after graduating. The degree didn't target specific skills for the workforce, so I copied most of my friends who specialized in something else related to science. I applied for further studies in audiology, optometry, physiotherapy and chiropractic as well as graduate programs with the National Australia Bank, Ernst & Young and PwC Australia. I applied for consulting roles with the government and even a technical role based in Antarctica. All of which I was rejected, either because my grades weren't high enough or I didn't pass the interview. One piece of feedback I remember from one interview was that my personality wasn't the right fit for the profession. Ironically years later a company rejected my job application not based on my skill set but rather on the results of an online personality test. It was demoralizing but I now understand why autism can be referred to as a personality disorder.

Eventually I did get accepted into a 2-year Radiation Therapy Masters course. In a tight cohort of sixteen students we learnt the planning and treatment skills to manage radiation therapy treatment for cancer patients. I really enjoyed the technical aspects of the job and the idea of helping sick people made me feel special. The entire second year was a full-time paid internship at a professional clinic, so by the end all of us were guaranteed to land a job. And by all of us I mean everyone except for me.

Three months away from graduating, my self-esteem took a sharp turn when the clinical manager, a man I had occasional reviews with, tapped me on the shoulder.

"Come with me," he said.

I looked up at his concerned face. Holding the door open he waited for me to take a seat in his office. I remember it was 5pm on a Friday and I wanted to go home.

"Is something wrong?" I said.

His face gave the impression he had bad news. Like you see in the movies when a police officer needs to tell someone one of their family members have just died. I sat with anticipation.

"Are you aware of ever having any learning difficulties?" he said.

I remember opening my mouth wanting to respond but nothing came out. His question caught me off-guard.

"We've noticed delays with your development, at the beginning you were progressing well but for some reason you've plateaued," he said.

I tried to keep my face straight. "Are you sure?" I replied.

He nodded and then spoke of examples where I failed to listen to instructions, asked questions about things previously mentioned, and asked things I was expected to already know. The tall man got worked up in frustration, stressing I had lots of catching up to do, otherwise he was going to fail me. I left the meeting very puzzled. "Am I not supposed to ask questions?" I thought.

For the past eight months I'd turned up every morning with a smile, cheerful with all the staff, never complained and was always happy to do the unwanted jobs. I was also highly regarded among other students and achieved distinction grades on the course theory. What went wrong? It appeared I had a great understanding of the job but couldn't apply the theory to the practical environment.

My enjoyment and motivation of working there dropped dramatically and within a week I was pulling my hair out. If I had a question, I wasn't sure whether to ask for fear of looking foolish. But if I never asked questions, I would only be guessing on what to do next. Due to the building pressure and high number of female staff, approaching questions also became a problem. "How do I ask politely?" I thought. At times ladies raised their voice in frustration or turned the other way when I headed in their direction. Things got worse when they phoned up my course coordinator who drove an hour out of her way to look over my shoulder. I saw her frown at the clinical educator, indicating she wasn't happy with them. I then overheard heated conversations between the pair blaming each other for my delayed development. At the time not I or anyone seemed to understand what was happening. I remember coming home one day, crunching myself up in a ball and just cried. I hated life. I wanted to drop out.

It wasn't until mum shared some insight about my youngest sibling Taylor when I believed the answer was found. Two years earlier she was diagnosed with dyslexia, a learning disorder that causes difficulties in reading, writing, spelling, speech and working memory skills. Once I heard the disorder runs in families, I immediately booked myself in for an assessment at the Alison Lawson Clinic. The clinic offers a simple, safe and successful treatment program for visual dyslexia.

I remember they tested my distance and near reading abilities as well as having a deeper look into my eyes using an ophthalmoscope. This is an instrument which looks like a torch and has unique lenses which can see all the way through to the back of the eyeball. My therapist made the following comments:

> *The results indicate that Travis has visual dyslexia with significant movement in the right macula. This is preventing him from being able to get steady fixation to read and retain information needed*

for short term memory processing, necessary for all literacy and numeracy skills.

This would result in an inability to hold and process information needed to complete written tasks and would cause him to read and re read information to try and gain an understanding of its content.

He has been using multiple strategies to gain and store information which would require excessive study and his achievements to date are a measure of his determination to succeed.

He is an ideal candidate for treatment and should obtain a positive outcome with improvements in his memory, reading ability and a broad range of skills and abilities reliant on a steady macula.

I remember shaking my head in disbelief. "Why wasn't this picked up earlier?"

The therapist praised me for finishing high school.

"You must be very determined," she said.

My parents and I didn't know how I survived for so long. Unlike my sister who sat through weekly reading recovery sessions with a tutor, I had somehow flown under the radar. Never did I read for pleasure. It takes an enormous amount of mental effort to read and comprehend information. As I look back now throughout school reading novels and other large texts felt like a chore which I'd try avoiding whenever possible. I wasn't the type to speak up, which didn't help my situation either. Quietly plowing through was the only way.

Interestingly, Taylor dropped out of high school in year 11 because she found the schoolwork all too hard. Academics has never been one of her strengths and she much prefers getting her hands dirty with manual labor jobs. Today she is happily working in the trades as a cabinet maker. I have no doubt she has other undiagnosed neurodevelopmental conditions which have contributed to her life decisions. She is also the only one in the family who laughs at my jokes and relates to my quirky sense of humor.

At the time I was reinvented with the new diagnosis and treatment plan, so I returned to work with a positive attitude. I believed my life was about to change. I now knew what the problem was so it could be managed, and hence steer me back on track to finish the course. However once several staff became aware of my dyslexia working at the clinic just wasn't the same.

CHAPTER TWENTY-SEVEN

"DO YOU WANT to clean the storeroom?" my clinical educator said.

The lady next to her raised her eyelids. I asked her to repeat the question even though I heard her the first time.

From my time working at the clinic over the past year, I'd never seen or heard anyone cleaning the storeroom. The building had used janitors who would come in after hours. I remember looking over at the three available computers behind her, but for some reason she refused to let me use them. At the time I needed as much practice as possible with the radiation planning software to sharpen my skills.

At first I didn't understand her reasoning and reluctantly grabbed the broom. Then after a few minutes of sweeping the dismal nature of the situation finally sunk in. "She thinks I'm incapable," I thought.

Tightening my grip on the handle I got angry, then with an overload of emotions I bashed the broom against the wall. For the next few minutes I was unable to control my behavior pacing around the room. Luckily no one heard me because I was cursing out loud, "Why can't I do this fucking job!" Once my clinical educator got word about the dyslexia, she'd lost faith in teaching me. Given the ongoing burden of struggling at work her discrimination that day tipped me over the edge. It's only now I look back and believe I'd had a meltdown. That is an intense response to an overwhelming situation where one loses control and lashes out verbally and/or physically. Many autistic people have them. And there's more to come in this story.

The site manager recognized the mistake and pulled my educator aside to organize an apology, preventing things getting out of control. However even afterwards the work environment just wasn't the same.

There was no way I could focus on finishing the course without second guessing myself and having awkward feedback conversations. Especially after the whole department became aware of my condition.

Not long after the incident I failed the final unit and deferred from the course whilst all my peers graduated, achieved their accreditation and gained full-time employment. I remember it was sickening. And the worst part was having to explain to them why I couldn't join the celebrations, the ones I'd helped organize. I was highly respected among my fellow students who would often come to me with questions. No one expected me to fail. And some didn't even believe me when I told them I was. At the time I was too confused and upset to share the truth around the dyslexia, so I said my grandfather had recently passed away and needed some time off. This was technically correct, my grandfather (the same one mentioned earlier) had actually passed away a few years earlier from prostate cancer.

Looking back now I wish I'd considered seeking professional help and even some legal advice around why I was failing. I hated the fact all my peers were graduating without me. In workplaces today, situations like this would be far better handled. People with hidden disabilities are better supported and entitled to more help.

Adding to the turmoil at the time, a bright girl I was dating had dumped me. One of many girls leaving me over the years but I regret the mistakes I made with this one. She was a high achieving journalism graduate with big career dreams to work internationally for the United Nations. I remember her charcoal skin turning pale.

"You treat me like a friend, not a girlfriend," she said.

I'd planned to attend a 21st birthday the same weekend she booked a romantic weekend away for us. For some reason even though they were a 2-hour drive apart I still attempted to attend both. It didn't go down well. Writing about it now I shake my head but that's how much of a people pleaser I was. The need to please and always say yes regardless of the circumstances is a common trait in those with ADHD.

The day after turning 24 I completed the program at the clinic, which was designed to stabilize the macula in my right eye. This involved lots of brain exercises such as word-finds, crosswords and sudoku puzzles which I completed in front of a rotating projector screen. The exercises were done wearing glasses with red and green lenses. The therapist said it would reactivate areas of my brain which had been lying dormant.

At the time I remember noticing improved alertness and a better ability to retain information. Similar to a software upgrade for a computer, the treatment allowed me to function with a faster processing speed. This motivated me to read more and practice my comprehension.

Here are my therapist's comments after completing the treatment program:

> *The final results show that the visual dyslexia has been cured and the right macula is steady, allowing for strong fixation at all levels.*
>
> *Travis is now able to read and hold information long enough for it to be processed in the short-term memory, which will allow him to achieve his full potential and succeed at university and in the workplace. There should also be a steady improvement in his comprehension, spelling and writing skills.*

Many people note a calming effect of the treatment as the macula is no longer moving. This may become even more apparent after the stress of the treatment exercises has ceased. Anxieties should ease and become less apparent in daily life.

I remember feeling revived. The extra confidence spurred me on to return to university the following year. I had unfinished business. Working at a new clinic with new staff provided a fresh start, where I could focus on the work without being reminded of previous trauma.

Six weeks in I was tracking well, passing all the assessments in the treatment department with high marks. However the work seemed much harder when I moved across into the planning department. Unlike treatment, there was no one to shadow, no routine or patterns of behavior I could follow. At times I found myself twiddling my thumbs, which was bizarre because I had a thorough knowledge of the job and knew what needed to be done but for whatever reason couldn't do it. Not unless someone told me where to start, and what to do next. I remember given three patient files, all of which were at different stages of planning. Two were classed as radical (life - saving) and the other palliative (pain – relief). I concentrated on the first radical patient because I wanted to save her life. She was also young, so it made sense to attend her first.

My new clinical educator peered over my shoulder with concern. I remember hearing her awkward scoff of disapproval.

"Why are you working on that patient now?" she said.

I stuttered, feeling remnants of deja vu. "The, the, this one was signed off by the doctor last week."

I pointed to the patients age of twenty-two. She irritably shook her head, then said the palliative patient was a more complicated setup and had been waiting much longer. I still disagreed. Even though she had over twenty years of experience in the field, nothing she said made sense. It's like we spoke two different languages. Why would I waste time working on a stage four elderly man who's only expected to live a few months, when I could be planning treatment to save the life of a young girl.

Things then went from bad to worse when I made an impulsive decision.

"Mum can I please borrow some money?" I said.

Around the same time two girls jet-setting overseas on a road trip around USA in a mustang convertible had invited me to join them. One of them was a friend I'd known for three years, the other I'd never met. Without a shadow of doubt I booked airfares roughly one week after I was due to complete the course. Even after failing last time I still didn't see the risk of cutting it fine. At the time I believed everything would work itself out. And it did, except for when my new educator was reporting back to the university. Her eyes filled with tears.

"Sorry, I have to fail you," she said.

"Fail me? Why?" I replied.

I sat there in shock as reality kicked in. Back then I couldn't understand. The way things ended the year before left me hungry with unfinished business. I was so close yet so far away from the finish line. Why was she failing me?

I remember she said there were still gaps in my planning skills and there wasn't enough time left to reach a level of competency. I was also still asking lots of questions around my daily activities and continually needed supervision. Many staff were not yet confidant in my abilities. Clearly I hadn't planned for developmental delays and assumed passing the final unit after eight months off would be a breeze.

At age twenty-five my life had hit this crossroad and I needed to make a choice. A choice that would steer my life into two very different directions. I could've stayed on an extra 2 – 3 months, got myself up to speed to graduate from the course I'd worked so hard on before entering the workforce. Or I could blow $12,000 jetting away to the USA with two attractive girls in a mustang convertible. A first world problem. What would you do? Researchers say by age twenty-five the human brain finishes its remodeling and development phase, however I don't believe this is true if you're neurodivergent.

CHAPTER TWENTY-EIGHT

I STILL REMEMBER the first time I met Fatemeh at a club one night. She was wearing these golden moon-shaped earrings with a hollow center that had four individual prongs, each holding a tiny diamond. Around her neck was a middle eastern scarf which I found out she had previously worn as a hijab. Captivated by her appearance I could tell she wasn't a local from the area. I've always been attracted to dark-skinned girls from foreign countries. To this day friends still poke fun about it.

After a drink or two I found the courage to find Fatemeh on the dance floor and turn on some moves.

"Are you from Saudi Arabia?" I said.

She pulled a distorted face and raised her middle finger. I flashed my palms, "Oh jeez I'm sorry."

She smiled, grabbed my hands then moved her hips closer. It must have been the alcohol. I chose to keep my mouth shut after that, except of course when we kissed. From that moment on I was all in.

While hustling and bumping around each other I managed to somehow take one of her earrings without her noticing. Rather than giving it back I decided to take it home and use it as an excuse for her to keep seeing me. My plan worked however once I returned the earring the romance between us fizzled and we just became good friends. Fatemeh migrated from Iran as a teenager and her parents sent her to a wealthy private girls' school. Given they were still living abroad I remember picking her up from school a few times and helping her with maths homework. She was definitely younger than me, but I never actually knew how much. Her date of birth had been forged on her passport to help get her into the country so I didn't know her real age. Back then it didn't bother me because she was far more confident and socially mature, which I really liked. I was also intrigued by her heavy Persian accent which she was skilled at using to get out of sticky situations. Her fluency was similar to Peter however when she spoke her jaw didn't move and her tongue seemed thick and flat inside her mouth adding an exotic monotone to her voice.

When Fatemeh and I hung out I was confused on where the boundaries were in our friendship. She enjoyed flashing her red credit card and offered paying for things.

"Aren't guys supposed to buy the girls drinks?" I said.

Her face mimicked Zoolander's blue steel. "I'm not like the other girls," she replied.

I remember buying her a Christmas present one time which included expensive jewelry and a framed picture of us from our day trip to the snow. She kissed me on the cheek. "That's so sweet of you!"

Back then I was ready to take our relationship to the next level but didn't quite know how. How do you bring it up? What do you say? Maybe we were dating at one point and I didn't realize. Fatemeh regularly messaged to ask what I was doing and invited me along on random road trips and adventurous activities. I always prioritized her and said yes. Strangely though, when I reached out to her she was usually busy or unavailable.

I look back and think part of me dropped out of university believing something magical would spark between us overseas. We'd be in each other's faces everyday so there was no way she could say she was busy. But while we were in the presence of her friend Jessamine, it created an annoying obstacle which was always getting in our way. I believe the slang word for this is "cockblock".

I'd never met Jessamine before the trip, only heard about her from Fatemeh. They went to school together and played violin. She was a chunky blonde brought up in the affluent suburbs of Sydney. Australian born from Russian parents she came across as opinionated and at times a bit snobbish. I still recall a comment she made when we were in the queue of an American bar, "They're letting her in and she's not even as pretty as me." Back then I was curious how on earth Jessamine could judge a girl based on her appearance after only looking at her for less than a minute. None of us had even spoken to her or introduced ourselves. Once inside, I decided to venture off and say hello to this girl while Fatemeh and Jessamine waited in line for the bathroom.

I remember this girl had a tattoo of a unicorn on the back of her neck. Tapping her on the shoulder I greeted her using dad's slang, "G'day mate, how are you going?"

She turned and chuckled, "Excuse me?"

One thing I learnt in the USA is the powerful first impression of the Australian accent. As soon as the girls returned, I showed them the new mobile number saved into my phone.

I turned to Jessamine and grinned. "I think she's pretty," I said.

Both girls bounced off their toes with energy.

"No way! Who was it, point her out now," Fatemeh said.

Once Jessamine realized it was the girl she had commented about earlier, all respect vanished into thin air. She shook her head. "Oh please tell me it's not her!"

Fatemeh also disapproved, raising the corner of her mouth.

"Bit creepy," she said.

I winked at her while Jessamine had her head down and dry reached. Fatemeh's pupils dilated with intrigue. The girl with the unicorn tattoo never actually gave me her number. I had created a fake one myself.

CHAPTER TWENTY-NINE

FOR THE FIRST week in the Mustang I'd been the girls' chauffeur, driving them all around California and shadowing their activities. Both said they were too afraid to take the wheel because everything was on the other side of the road. At first I didn't mind however after six weeks of driving through Canada and Nebraska I realized it turned me bitter. Looking back I wish I better understood the workload before signing up.

Over the course of our trip Fatemeh and Jessamine constantly reminded me of things I wasn't doing. Leaving the toilet seat up, forgetting to use my manners and owing them money for shared expenses were the most common. "You forgot again!" they would say.

I remember responding with a kindhearted, "ok" but it only raised tensions further. Especially with regards to money from Jessamine. She accused me of forgetting on purpose to avoid paying but it wasn't true. I simply had trouble keeping track of all the expenses, what I'd already paid and what I'd owed. Fatemeh warned me to double check in case I'd paid Jessamine for the same thing twice. Overall, it was difficult to be myself and enjoy the trip without breaking eggshells and receiving criticism.

There were times when the girls asked for my input on where

to go and what to do and I'd simply shrug saying, "I don't know". It was like I had my own unrelatable interests. For example, I remember wanting to appeal our parking fine in a Seattle court room, book tickets to a Nicki Minaj concert, roll down a Canadian hill in a bob sled and regularly eat out at the same takeaway food outlets. When I'd suggest my ideas to the girls all I got was silence. The trip reached a point where I was looking for any excuse to be alone.

"I have more fun by myself," I said.

It was a hard pill for the girls to swallow. On one occasion in a Las Vegas shopping centre I waited for them to turn around, then simply ran away. Like a dog in a park without a leash I was free to enjoy the rest of the day on my terms. But when the owner becomes aware of his dog's bad behavior there's always conflict.

Jessamine's eyebrows furiously furrowed. "Where the hell did you go?" she said.

I answered with a pause and a higher vocal pitch, making it sound like a question, "For a, walk."

Her volume lifted. "That was 6 hours ago! We're girls, you can't just leave us by ourselves in a foreign country!"

Fatemeh stood next to her crossing her arms in solidarity. Given our history she was more sympathetic, but this time it was clear I'd crossed the line. They both shouted at me as I shrugged, not knowing what to say.

"I don't think he understands," Jessamine said.

Fatemeh flexed her lower eyelids, looking me up and down.

"Yeah, have you got something?" she said.

At the time I thought she was asking me for money. Only later on did I realize what she really meant. For days after I questioned her judgement thinking she must be insane. Did I have something? What exactly did I have and what was giving her that impression? Little did I know the girls were onto something big. They could detect something wasn't quite right but none of us had any explanation, so we were simply left dumbfounded.

Due to the rising tensions between us we organized a meeting. I remember crouching inside the mustang late at night for a two hour heavy confrontation. The girls spoke about my lack of communication and disrespectful behavior, red flagging my refusal to share food in an Asian restaurant, times when I left behind rubbish, eating before going out for dinner with friends, failing to show appreciation or gratitude and not speaking up with my feelings.

"It's important for relationships," they said.

The girls lectured me on life and said I needed to change. Back then it was my fault for the ongoing drama. At the time I didn't entirely agree or understand with some of the things they were saying but kept it to myself. Today with a better understanding of autism and ADHD, I can certainly see where their feedback was coming from. I wish I could hop inside a DeLorean and travel back to this moment. I wish I could share with them what I know now about my neurodivergent conditions. Things would have been much different. The trip would have run smoother. Life would have been so much easier.

I remember only ten days into the trip I was miserable and regretted my decision to travel with them. Had I'd known the trip would turn into an episode of Trav does the darndest things, I would've stayed home and finished off my university course.

Our discussions inside the mustang escalated as my lips drooped.

"I don't want to travel with you girls anymore, can I leave?" I said.

Fatemeh gasped with shock. "If you leave us, our friendship is over."

At the time her response didn't make any sense. Even though I still had a crush on her, we weren't dating. She also still had Jessamine who seemed half pleased I might be leaving. We could all meet at the airport for our return flight home then share stories of our separate adventures. It made sense to me.

Weighing up the options in my head I was unsure I could survive another month under their surveillance. I wanted to do my own thing but at the same time didn't want to upset Fatemeh or damage friendships. I felt trapped. I wanted to run away but had nowhere to go.

From this experience I've learnt confrontation with girls is highly complex and requires a completely different set of skills. With Scott and Bart I had better grasp on what they were throwing in my direction and how it would impact me. For example when Bart punched me in the face, I knew he wanted to hand me a swollen jaw for lying to him but when the girls say something it could mean a variety of different things. Their words might sound fine but the way they say it could sound unpleasant or condescending.

My head throbbed listening and trying to absorb everything the girls were saying. They spoke with speed, fluency and a colorful array of tones I desperately tried to decode. I remember not knowing how to respond with all the hidden meanings.

Whenever one would gesture with an eyebrow, a squint, a mouth shrug, a lip purse or a change in pitch the other would replicate with ease. They laughed at each other's humor and shared the same opinions about everything. It was like they were harmoniously on the same channel, and I was constantly pressing buttons on the remote, searching for the right tune.

My vocal cords rattled. "I don't like being told what to do," I said.

The girls laughed. Eventually our meeting swung towards some understanding once I was able to communicate how I felt. It was agreed I would put in more effort to address the issues. By the end the tension had dissipated, and we all wrapped arms. I remember leaning in with pouted lips thinking something romantic was about to happen. I wanted to seize the opportunity. Fatemeh pulled the door handle.

"Where are you going?" I said.

She laughed. I will remember the night in the mustang for

the rest of my life. The discussions with the girls were intense. So intense that none of us even realized we had parked in a permit zone. The following day, we discovered the car had been towed. Luckily Fatemeh was able to have it released and paid the infringement on her credit card.

"I will just tell them our car was stolen," she said.

To my dismay there was no romance between Fatemeh and I on the trip and after returning to Australia we sadly drifted apart. From what I see on social media she is now married with two children. Last I heard Jessamine is still single. This doesn't surprise me.

CHAPTER THIRTY

SCARRED BY MY experiences with the girls it was a few years before I travelled with other people again. I learnt the hard way travelling requires planning and a robust awareness of your environment and surroundings. Both inside and outside your body. This is critical for safety and survival. Developing this skill paved the way for more bombshell overseas adventures, like the time I visited Sri Lanka.

A group of us had flew over there to celebrate the wedding of one of our friends. I remember shrieking with excitement when asked to be a groomsman. For me it was a no brainer. It's not every day you're invited to an overseas wedding, but I'll never understand why many people have second thoughts and often turn down these rare opportunities.

Carly and I walked along the Sri Lankan foreshore. I remember being completely captivated by the foreign surroundings, running my hand through the hot sand, breathing in the smell of burning wood and examining the widespread litter, local shanties and people gawking at our white faces.

Carly and I were mutual friends with the groom and only met a handful of times before the trip. As a qualified social worker she was very kind, thoughtful and had a sarcastic sense of humor. We've never had any romantic history however are still good friends today. Interestingly she too has been diagnosed with ADHD.

Wiping my sweaty face with a handkerchief she handed me a bottle. "Would you like some water?" Carly said.

The side of my mouth raised into a smirk. "Nah, I can rehydrate with a beer."

We stopped at a KFC on our way back to the hotel.

"What would you like to drink sir?" the cashier said.

Without any hesitation I nodded, "Coke please."

Two hours later the fatigue kicked in. Then the dizziness. I remember looking at my watch thinking it was far too early for bed. Like an old man in a retirement village, I palmed my mate's bedroom door.

"I don't feel right," I said.

He wailed. Earlier in the day he'd fallen ill from eating street food so he wasn't of much help. Carly had also stayed out with our other mates exploring more of the city. My body trembled walking down the stairs to hotel reception. The staff grimaced.

"Are you ok?" they said.

Losing balance I gripped tightly onto the bench. "I need to see a doctor," I replied.

I remember my tuk tuk driver looked like a brown version of Steve Irwin. When he saw me his eyelids widened like he'd been frightened by a ghost.

"Are you dengue?" he said.

I couldn't be bothered with the language barrier so I nodded. At the time in Sri Lanka there was an outbreak of dengue fever, a flu-like virus spread by mosquitos.

The ends of his long hair tickled my face as we flew down the road dodging heavy traffic.

He pointed to the emergency door outside Durdans Hospital.

"I stay here!" he said.

I pulled out my wallet to pay him, but he refused.

"You don't have to," I replied.

He shook his head then repeated, "I stay here!"

I started freaking out in the waiting room when my symptoms got worse. My vision was as blurry as an alcoholic, and I had trouble making a fist. I remember a nurse touching my arm and expressing concern, "Ok?" she said.

Luckily the doctor spoke better English, "Why are you here?" he said.

"I think I might have dengue," I replied.

Facing the wall he typed on his 1980s box-like computer while I answered questions.

Only minutes passed before I froze. Then my body shook, then my teeth chatted. I felt cold like I was standing naked out in the Antarctic. I interrupted the doctor, belching like Barney Gumble from the Simpsons.

"I don't feel so good," I said.

I remember the wheels from his chair screeching on the floor when he quickly turned. Then with a sense of urgency he raised his voice and said in his thick accent "Don faint!"

The next thirty seconds are blurry, but I still recall the intense fear for my life. I thought I was going to die, if not from dengue fever some other hospital infection. Imagine three tiny nurses dragging a large white man along the floor of their hospital, then hoisting him into an ICU bed. I was told afterwards I had attracted an audience. My room reminded me of a bunk house inside a backpacker hostel. Here is a picture of me on the IV drip.

Kudos to my friend Nick Dunn for taking the photo.

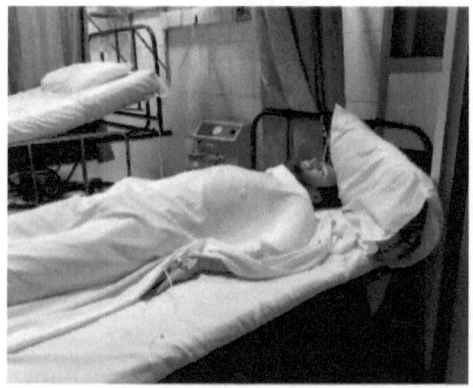

When I opened my eyes the first thing I saw was a mosquito. If my back wasn't in pain from the rocky mattress I would've fainted again. It is incredibly disturbing how unequipped hospitals are in developing countries overseas. We're so lucky in Australia.

Without any restraint my tuk tuk driver gushed into the room. "Take dis," he said.

Freaked out by his energy I looked over at the concerned nurse trying to get his attention. I blocked his arm with my elbow as the driver reached for my mouth.

"You're not a doctor!" I said.

"Make you feel better," he replied.

Another nurse finally entered the room and confirmed the tablet was only Panadol. I took the pill then shut my eyes. Within the hour the word had spread, and my room was surrounded with visitors which included the bride, groom, the bride's parents, a cousin, my bridal partner Nethu and two others from the bridal party. I had stolen the attention away from the wedding which was now only two days away.

The bride's father touched my hand. "We're getting you transferred to a better hospital," he said.

At the time I wasn't totally sure I could trust him, but anything was better than the mosquito net. Ironically the father worked as a salesman selling asbestos to construction companies. I'd never heard anyone doing that job before, for obvious reasons.

"I take him," my tuk tuk driver replied.

Someone turned to the driver and frowned. Luckily my wheelchair didn't fit inside his tuk tuk.

The Wellawatta hospital was far more professional. All the staff wore uniforms, it had clean ventilation, no insects and their beds were comfortable. I can only look back now and laugh the building was likely insulated with asbestos.

Within a few hours I regained some energy, hopeful to be fit enough for the wedding.

The doctor returned with my blood results. "No dengue fever, but I need you to drink more water," he said.

I touched the side of my forehead and dipped my chin in shame.

When I got back to the hotel my friends laughed. The entire time I was simply dehydrated but had no idea.

"Weren't you thirsty?" someone asked.

I threw my hands in frustration, "I don't even know!"

The timing of this incident was just enough to recover before the wedding. I remember laying low under the hotel air conditioner and stocking up on hydrolytes. The wedding itself was memorable and we were all treated like celebrities. It wasn't hard to pick out the white faces amongst the locals. All the bride's relatives knew what had happened because they'd pitched in to cover the cost of my hospital fees. I offered to pay them back but they wouldn't accept. Interestingly the hospital fees in Sri Lanka were still less than the excess cost on my Australian travel insurance.

I remember the hospital incident also sparked a romantic interest with Nethu. We were paired up for the traditional dance. She was a family friend of the brides. She had these beautiful hands covered with henna tattoo designs and long fingernails. I remember being mesmerized as she twirled her wrists to the sounds of the classical native instruments.

After the wedding celebrations Nethu pulled me aside and smiled.

"Come with me, I have a gift for you," she said.

Without a second thought I followed her into a tuk tuk which drove us to a large Buddhist temple.

"Let's pray," she said.

I'd never prayed before, so I remember looking around the room for someone else to copy. I had no idea what I was doing so I clasped my hands together like a steeple and rested them against my chest.

She giggled. "Close your eyes."

Kneeling in front of the statue she placed a bracelet made from white cotton around my wrist, then whispered kind words into my ear, "It will keep you safe."

I can still feel the hot air from her mouth melting inside my ear. In that moment I felt like I was on cloud nine. I remember a pleasurable tingling sensation on my skin running down the back of my neck. On our return home, the back seat of the tuk tuk transformed into a kissing booth. Oblivious to the exposures of heavy traffic pollution and roaring engine noises around us, Nethu and I showcased first base like nothing else in the world mattered. It was a happy ending to a traumatic trip.

One might think living through a dehydration experience like this is a one off. i.e. You only make the mistake once. But four years later it happened again in Australia. I forgot to drink water after a 5km run. I remember the doctor asking me if I was on drugs. If only the penny dropped earlier, I could've saved myself the overnight stay in hospital and the $500 bill.

CHAPTER THIRTY-ONE

UNEXPECTED LEARNING AND behavioral problems continued to emerge throughout my history of employment. This made it harder not only to choose the right job for my skill set but also commit to one long term.

Throughout my twenties I had a variety of different jobs across different workplaces and industries, most of which didn't last any longer than a few months. Among them were carrying plates in hospitality, appearing as an extra in a television series, serving alcohol at festivals and driving a tractor to collect hay on regional country farms. Given my tertiary education I was overqualified and underpaid. At the time I knew this but didn't know what I wanted to do or how I could possibly get there. As you're aware I'd already tried to finish my radiotherapy course and failed, twice.

I remember my younger brother Jack was accepted into a Pharmacy course and I quickly became interested in following suite. Jack had provided the answer for me. Or did he?

Initially my plan was to gain experience working with Pharmacists in a retail store for entry into the course. It turned out to be the most memorable of all my jobs. Fast paced, I was constantly bombarded with customers, asking questions, negotiating pricing and health fund discounts while providing advice to meet their needs around the selling of prescription and over the counter medicines.

On busy days I remember coming home and collapsing on the couch, fatigued with a drained social battery. Even today it is still the most taxing job I've ever had.

I enjoyed helping 99% of the customers who came in. Most of the time I avoided the other 1% because I could see they were aggressive. I've never known how to deal with aggressive people. Avoiding them was impossible though on days when the store was under-staffed. I had no choice. The store had narrow aisles stockpiled to the brim with thousands of products. Everyone regularly got in each other's way, especially me. For some reason I found it hard to make it from point A to point B without accidently bumping a customer, tripping over my own toes or side stepping in the right direction to avoid an awkward collision. There didn't appear to be any safe zones however I'll never forget one night when I was forced to run away.

A large European lady approached me while I was filling the shelf with anti-inflammatories. She handed me a pair a sunglasses with a lens popped out.

"Hey you, I need to return these," she said.

"Oh what happened," I replied.

She immediately unleashed her frustration saying the lens fell out during her morning walk with the dog. She breathed heavily with disapproval. "You sell cheap and nasty products here!"

"Do you have the receipt?" I said.

She shook her head. "You only sold them to me last week!"

I couldn't remember serving her but the frame was one I'd seen on the shelf before. Irritated by her attitude I looked down at the frame and pondered. Being the problem solver that I am I wanted to fix them right there in front of her. The hole cut out appeared stretched or warped which for some reason was too big to fit the lens. When I showed this to her she replied negatively, "Yeah I know that already, just fix it now or give me a refund please."

Looking back I should've said no, especially since she didn't have a receipt but at the time my strong desire to solve problems got the better of me. I also didn't know how to say no to her without making things worse. She was a strong opinionated lady who seemed used to getting her own way. Being able to say no to someone was a social skill I hadn't learned yet which made the customer service work even harder.

"I have an idea," I said.

I went out the back and carefully placed a tiny drop of super glue inside the frame, then holding the lens in place I dried it under the electronic hand dryer in the bathroom. Impressed with my creative efforts I returned with a smile.

"Here you are!" I said.

She snatched the sunglasses from my hands and lifted them up to her face. I watched with confusion as this lady examined them from different angles. It was as if she was looking through a microscope trying to pick out any faults. Then like a magpie about to swoop her eyes widened.

"What's this?" she said.

"The lens," I replied.

The lady then raised her voice pointing to something in the corner,

"No, this!"

I remember noticing a tiny discoloration on the edge of the lens, roughly the size of a strand of hair. I shrugged. She stamped her foot in frustration, making a scene.

"It wasn't there before!" she said.

The tension increased. I raised one eyebrow and listened to her accuse me of selling her cheap and nasty sunglasses. She was technically right our sunglasses collection wasn't great but what did she expect. It was a pharmacy. Everyone knows to shop at sunglass stores for better quality sunglasses. I remember wanting to quote the ads from television and say, "should've gone to Specsavers" but was too scared.

"I'm not leaving until you fix this," she said.

I stared at her unfriendly face and sighed, not knowing what to say. She wore a thick layer of makeup over her hardened features. She looked like one of those ladies who'd had a rough life with multiple ex-husbands. Looking back now my face probably looked guilty but at the time I didn't feel guilty and hand on heart didn't believe I'd done anything wrong. It was possible I may have accidently marked the lens and not realized but in the moment all I could focus on was this lady's hysteric behavior. As a result of my undiagnosed conditions, I didn't know how to defend myself. I didn't know how to smooth things over or say the right things to satisfy her and make her go away.

I couldn't issue a refund for her either because the system wouldn't allow it without a receipt. Rattled and confused I took the glasses behind the counter.

"What's the matter?" a colleague said.

I frowned and stared helplessly down at the floor.

"Where's the boss?" I replied.

At the time he was out the back on a smoke break. The situation escalated when the lady made a phone call. "Hey! Someone wants to speak with you, he's not happy."

Twice I refused on taking the phone, but the lady was persistent. I remember a part of me was also curious on who she called and why they might want to talk to me. Holding it next to my ear I remember feeling the onset of another meltdown. The man had a deep European accent more aggressive than his female counterpart.

"What the fuck have you done to my sunnies?" he said.

I stood up on my tippy toes hot in the face.

"You listen to me!" I said.

By this point all eyes were on me. Every other customer and

staff member watched with anticipation as I walked out the store stuttering into the phone. Every time I spoke, the man spoke over the top using foul language, "Don't you lie, don't you lie, you fucking broke them!"

I remember it being impossible to get a full sentence in without being interrupted. Infuriated by the conversation I felt there was no choice but to hang up on him. I then went around the corner taking a moment to collect my thoughts. The phone continued to buzz but I didn't answer. I couldn't listen to anymore abusive nonsense. Sitting there I remember questioning why these two people were attacking me. The customer had come to me with broken sunglasses and no receipt, and I went out of my way to help them. I just couldn't understand.

Back then I was convinced they were in the wrong and given how much they upset me, there were thoughts of revenge. Luckily, I had already learnt the consequences of doing that years earlier with Scott and Bart. When I returned the lady was sitting in the prescription waiting area holding a pen and paper with crossed arms. Her nostrils flared. "Write your name, date, time and a note saying what you've done." Finally my boss arrived,

"Is everything ok?" he said.

I shook my head in dismay and shed a tear. I couldn't deal with it so without speaking another word I returned the lady's phone and walked out of the store a second time. Only this time I hopped in my car and drove off. I remember still having two hours left to go in my shift but I didn't care. In the moment all I wanted to do was run away and never go back.

Fuming at myself behind the wheel I knew there was only one thing I could do to make myself feel better. Exercise. On my way home I pulled over at an oval and sprinted four laps then smashed out 50 push-ups. The whole time I was thinking if I don't get fired, I was going to quit.

The large European lady had filed a complaint against me but as it turned out I had support from other staff who told my boss the lady was a total bitch. Luckily this as well as my track record of never calling in sick was enough for him to keep me on the roster. The situation never escalated any further after the lady was awarded another pair of sunglasses for free. This was disappointing to hear but at the end of the day the most important thing remained. My dream of getting into Pharmacy was kept alive, however not for long.

CHAPTER THIRTY-TWO

THE PHARMACY HAPPENED to be located in one of the low-socioeconomic areas of Sydney and as a result attracted a variety of characters. Many of whom probably had more problems than me. I didn't realize this until well after landing the job!

I remember a time when a customer asked me to purchase their medication for them using my own debit card, saying they would pay me back. Another time a lady came in with her dog and toddler. The toddler walked alongside her wearing a dog leash around his neck while the dog was tucked in under a blanket like a baby inside a pram.

Dealing with difficult customers is hard enough but dealing with difficult staff is even worse. It's much harder to run away from them!

For a few months I worked with a troublemaker called Tyson. His personality and demeanor reminded me of Imani. Whenever he spoke, I couldn't tell if he actually meant what he was saying or whether it was just a fabrication of the truth. He also had an older sister who happened to be a hotshot lawyer which he enjoyed reminding us about. At first, I thought he was overly proud but later on someone told me he'd said he was using her to take advantage of his entitlements. It explained the extended lunch breaks, calling in sick last minute and overspending his annual leave. This often had a domino effect on everyone else needing to work harder to get the job done.

Once I realized this, I didn't like it because it was unfair. And for some unknown reason my boss never fired him. I've always had a strong sense of justice and when something is not right, I want to fix it. Even now while there are countries around the world being invaded, I have thoughts of wearing a cape and rising up, putting a stop to the killing of innocent civilians and the wars. One time I had a dream about convincing all the oligarchs in Russia to rise up against their dictator Vladimir Putin.

Tyson was a stocky blonde migrating from the Netherlands during his teens and worked at the pharmacy part time while studying at university. Ironically it was the same university as me and we even had a couple of mutual friends. One of the girls I knew had even dated him for a short time which apparently ended in a mess after he had cheated. It seemed as though wherever he went he left a trail of bad memories, kind of like a bad smell that won't go away.

I remember the period of time when our sales figures weren't adding up with the amount of cash found in the till. My boss thought some of us may have been accidently charging customers the wrong amount or forgetting to take payment. Mistakes happen from time to time but it wasn't until the night I was left in charge when shit hit the fan. It was simply out of my control.

Bianca, one of the female staff wiped her face with tears of despair.

"My fifty dollars is gone!" she said.

I looked up at the clock in surprise. She wasn't due back from her break for another twenty minutes.

Ever since first meeting her she was an emotional lady who struggled to make ends meet. I remember she liked to share dramatic stories about her two children which she cared for on her own.

There was one time her daughter was rushed to hospital after getting her head stuck in between the electric window of their car. She was the oldest and longest serving staff member among us and one everyone very much liked and respected. Anytime one of us needed help she was always there to lend a hand. No one likes losing money but if anyone needed it, it was Bianca. I'd often hear her complain she didn't have enough to buy her next packet of cigarettes.

The night she approached me in hysterics about her missing $50 note I felt sorry for her. I remember pausing thinking of something clever to say.

"Maybe you spent it," I replied.

She moaned and dipped her head into her hands. As I've seen from watching dad, money is like water and very easy to forget where it's spent. This seemed like the most logical explanation however Bianca wasn't impressed.

We headed for the staff room passing Tyson on the way who was speaking with another customer. Out of the corner of my eye I noticed he immediately left his seat to join us after seeing Bianca was upset.

"What's wrong?" he said.

I remember his hands nervously fidgeted then he insisted he wanted to help Bianca search the staff room for the missing $50 note.

"Aren't you busy with the customer?" I replied.

Tyson abruptly looked the other way.

"Oh, he's fine, why don't you mind the front for us," he said.

I have never been great at caring for girls, especially those who are upset so at the time I was happy to let them go. Looking back now though it was certainly a mistake.

Minutes later Tyson came back stretching open his wallet upside down with both hands. I remember he said my name in a creepy Count Dracula voice. His hands shook like he had Parkinson's and his face looked dead cold. Back then I wondered if he was having a seizure. I could've presented him with an Oscar that night. His voice quivered. "Someone has taken my ten dollars!"

I scratched my head getting flustered. It happened to be my first night filling in as manager and I wanted to impress the boss. After all the plan was to ask him to be my referee, in support of my application into the Pharmacy course.

Taking a moment to comprehend the situation I thought of all the possible things I could say to calm things down.

"Maybe you spent it," I said.

Tyson wasn't impressed then stuttered, "No, it was here!"

After we verified nothing was taken from my bag I thought whether the two were playing a trick on me, but Bianca looked too distraught.

"I'm calling the boss," she said.

Tyson replied impulsively. "I'll go with you!"

I pointed at Tyson's customer who was reading a brochure by himself.

"He'll be fine," Tyson said.

I remember thinking the situation was strange. Only the three of us and the Pharmacist were rostered on that night. The Pharmacist never leaves their station and I certainly didn't steal their money. Surely a customer wouldn't sneak into the staff room out the back and sift through our bags without being seen.

The following week Tyson made a comment out of the blue. "I hope no money goes missing today."

I stared at him closely through the mirror while he sprayed on his playboy cologne. Something didn't feel right with him.

A few days later our boss held a staff meeting to discuss another $250 cash missing from the till. He threw his pen on the floor and raised his voice,

"I'm pissed off! Over my 10 years here I've never had this happen before!" he said.

He was usually a cool and calm man, even in the face of aggressive customers. When I saw the steam coming off my boss's forehead, I blamed myself for his pain. Money had disappeared the night I was in charge therefore in my eyes I'd let him down, which unwittingly made me take on the responsibility of solving the crime. There was no reward, I simply wanted to be the hero and save the day.

From my bedroom I phoned my boss the next day, describing my version of events of the eventful night with Tyson and Bianca.

"You're now the second person who's said Tyson," my boss said.

Back then I had no idea but apparently Bianca also believed Tyson had stolen her money.

The penny suddenly dropped.

"That little weasel," I said.

"Yeah, we'll have to be more careful around him from now on," my boss replied.

He expressed his disgust of Tyson's behavior, and I shared a time Tyson asked to borrow twenty dollars from me to cover his Kris Kringle present for our Christmas party. I never saw my money again. My voice turned dark.

"Can you please get rid of him?" I said.

"Unfortunately mate without any proof there isn't much we can do,"

I remember throwing a pillow across my bedroom, distressed with his answer.

"It looks like he's gotten away with it this time. From now on no more storing cash in the till," my boss said.

Back then I didn't understand. After all the evidence I shared with him as well as Bianca coming forward, Tyson was allowed to walk away with over $500. My boss didn't question him or escalate the situation any further. He hoped given the hype from the meeting and new staff awareness; no more money would go missing.

The situation replayed over and over in my head and I couldn't let it go. At the time I was dating a bright girl by the name of Chaturi who was studying to become a doctor. I served her in the

Pharmacy one day before chasing her down the shopping center to get her number. I was attracted to her jet-black hair and introverted nerd personality.

I remember venting to her about the Tyson situation at work.

"Why do you care so much? It's not even your money" she said.

The problem was I was constantly reminded of it every time I saw his face at work. He appeared to be cheerful which only irritated me further. It was eating away at my soul.

One day I pulled Bianca aside to dig for information.

"Do you think Tyson stole your money?" I said.

Her eyes lit up. I could tell she needed to get it off her chest.

"Yes! I don't feel comfortable around him at all. You know when something doesn't feel right," she replied.

I nodded in agreement. Apparently on the night Tyson had grabbed the phone from Bianca while she was speaking to the boss. He then rudely interjected and said he'd had money stolen too. Bianca thought she was going crazy and no one would believe her. She felt sad and alone. Looking back on this moment it is right here when my undiagnosed autism hijacks my body and pulls me towards retribution. Just like Scott, Bart, Imani and Rohan, my brain had categorized Tyson as an enemy, and I simply couldn't sit back and do nothing.

My right arm extended and rested on Bianca's shoulder. I smirked.

"Let's get it back for you," I said.

She nervously held her breath then lowered her voice. "What are you going to do?"

CHAPTER THIRTY-THREE

I REMEMBER OUR store had a computer which stored the details of every customer and staff member dating back to when it first opened. The computer looked very similar to the 1980s box I saw right before I fainted in Sri Lanka. It was large, bulky and used a very outdated MS-DOS operating system. You had to enter in a password for access, but this was printed out and stuck on below the monitor. Anyone could easily log in.

During one of my shifts when the coast was clear I searched for Tyson's profile and jotted down his details. Later I then headed to a public phone booth dressed like a cat burglar. It was dark and breezy. I remember wearing a navy-blue hoodie. Looking back now I didn't need to go to so much effort. There was no chance anyone would recognize me.

My fingers punched the number buttons inside the phone booth with force. "Please return the money!" I typed.

After sending Tyson the text message I remember driving home laughing and singing songs of Mariah Carey. I've always had a soft spot for her music.

The next day I received a call from an excited Bianca.

"Hey guess what!" she said.

Tyson had called her in a hysteric panic only minutes after receiving my message. His words being, "You don't think it was me, do you? Because I had money stolen too!"

With big smiles on our faces we laughed together with incredible joy. Unfortunately, Chaturi didn't share this same joy and was rather surprised. Her dark face frowned with contempt.

"I can't believe you did that." she said.

It is here when I should've taken on board her feedback and put an end to my childish behavior but the hope and sheer will of getting everyone's money back was too overpowering. Bianca and I believed it was only a matter of time before Tyson's anxiety would get the better of him and there'd be no choice but for him to come clean. Sadly as the days passed nothing happened. So I sent him another message, repeating the same words. Still nothing.

Bianca convinced another two staff Tyson was behind the theft but neither of us had any solid proof. I remember this frustrated me. I'd made it my mission to get everyone's money back. Over the course of a few weeks it was all I ever thought about. Just like my high school revenge on Scott and Bart it had become my obsession, my special interest. There was no way I could accept Tyson sifting through people's bags and unlocking registers without being punished.

I tried planting a trap, leaving out my wallet with some money in an unzipped pocket for him to steal but he never took the bait. So I dived back into the computer and compiled a list of Tyson's close contacts, including his sister (the lawyer) and father. As I write this I'm shaking my head in disappointment with myself. Back then in my mid-twenties I just didn't know when to quit.

Leaning over and glaring down at the grid of telephone buttons I pressed the following, "Please tell Tyson to return the money!"

The plan was to spread the word at regular times every week. Applying pressure from different directions and backing him into a corner until he confessed. I was confident this plan would work like a charm. His sister would probe him and help bring him to justice. But I was wrong and unfortunately things backfired on me. I remember the night my boss called me with a strong sense of urgency.

"No more!" he said.

"What?" I replied.

"Look I know it's you! Stop messaging Tyson alright."

Like a dog being told off for bad behavior I winced.

"But he's stealing everyone's money," I replied.

Tyson and his sister had confronted my boss earlier that day and shown all the messages on their phones from an unknown sender. Apparently, they were appalled. The sister even said they were working with Police to investigate where the messages were sent from. Straight away my boss knew I was involved.

"Look, do you have any physical proof? A picture, video, anything?"

I wish I did but at the time all I could do was hang my head in shame. My boss chuckled and was amused by all the effort I went to. "You can't go around sending messages mate, you better drop it now before this turns ugly."

Looking back I was lucky my boss didn't go harder on me. As a result of my actions he was put in a very difficult position. Deep down I knew he was on my side and had great respect for my reliability and work ethic.

After our conversation I never sent anymore messages, even though I desperately wanted to. The police never reached out to me either. I'd made sure to cover my tracks sending the messages from different payphones nearby Tyson's house. I figured it might make him a suspect in his own case if they traced the locations.

Not long after the incident Tyson left to work at another store. Our Pharmacy was part of a large franchise with multiple sites around Sydney. He made a clean getaway with all the money. Even though I moved on years ago it still upsets me to this day. It wouldn't surprise me if he stole money from other pharmacies too.

I've come to learn the struggle to let things go and move forward is a common problem for those on the spectrum. It links back to having a superior long-term memory which in this case I think is more of a burden than an advantage.

Another common problem is finding the right job/career for your skill set. Even after all the dramas my boss was still kind enough to be my referee. But whatever he said, sadly it wasn't enough for entry into the pharmacy course. Just like that I was back to square one.

CHAPTER THIRTY-FOUR

BEING BLINDSIDED BY my conditions has led me to spend more time in hospital than most others my age. Like everything else in my life it seems to happen without warning, which sounds terrible but sometimes going to hospital can be a blessing in disguise.

One weekend in June I was at my parents' place, when I suddenly announced to dad I wanted to order a bowel screening kit.

He sipped beer from his favorite pewter mug.

"Why do you want to do that for?" he said.

Over the years I learned to filter out his feedback on his drinking nights. He'd stumble on his words and say strange things like he wanted to lose weight and become a professional footballer. Another time he said he wanted to be an artist and learn to speak French.

"So is that why you smoke?" I'd say.

We'd roll our eyes and laugh. You might think someone with atrial fibrillation who's had triple bypass surgery on their heart would be mindful of health and strongly in favor of getting things checked out. Not dad. He was unique. I remember the first thing he asked the nurse after waking up from one of his operations was, "When can I have a beer?" This time he recently had polyps removed during a colonoscopy, so the bowel topic was front of mind. For me anyway.

Luckily, I ignored his advice because my bowel screening results came back with traces of blood in my sample. I was then referred to a surgeon for further investigation.

"Do you have any symptoms?" he said.

I shook my head. He raised his eyebrows at my young age. "You're an outlier, and don't meet any criteria saying you need a colonoscopy."

At the time I was thirty-three and bowel screening didn't become a concern until age fifty, when the government post out your free test kit. He mentioned there was a 25% chance of error with the results and at the time I didn't have health insurance, which meant I needed to wear the full cost of the procedure.

"Let me think about it," I said.

From early teenage years I've been a big eater, sometimes not knowing when to stop. After finishing a restaurant meal I'd look around the table desperately waiting for family members to put down their cutlery. For a long time I also followed a regular morning routine of 6-7 Weet-Bix mashed with banana and doused in full cream milk. Diet is highly dependent on our brain because it signals to us what, when and how much to eat in response to feelings of hunger. And one needs to know how hungry they are to decide on how much to eat.

Two weeks later I was sitting inside a hospital waiting room wearing a gown, surrounded by elderly patients. They were all glued to the television watching the morning show while I played on my phone. My nurse raised an eyebrow. "What are you doing here? You're a bit young to be having a colonoscopy."

I sighed at the thought of wasting my time and throwing money away. I'd already wasted enough on unnecessary university fees that were accumulating with interest. However when I woke from the anesthetic the nurse's tone completely changed. "Are you ok? You've been out for a while."

"What day is it?" I replied.

My twenty minute colonoscopy took an hour as the surgeon needed to remove sixteen polyps, nine of which were classed as adenomas. These are the aggressive precancerous tumors which often grow into cancer if left untreated. At my age of 33 having this many is unheard of. The surgeon looked concerned.

"You made me work today. I need to see you again in three months," he said.

It wasn't until after the following colonoscopy when alarm bells rang. The surgeon removed another nine polyps, all of which were again adenomas. His eyes looked stern.

"I think you might have an FAP," he said.

My stomach dropped. I panicked at the sight of his serious face, thinking he was about to tell me how much longer I had left to live.

Familial Adenomatous Polyposis (FAP) is a rare genetic condition whereby the inner cells of the colon continuously form cancerous masses. Without surgical removal of the bowel, a person's life expectancy is significantly reduced.

Within only a few months my situation escalated from let's try a bowel screening test to waiting in horror for the results of genetic screening. This involved a series of blood tests along with an investigation into my family history. The results would determine the fate of my life. I remember being totally freaked out. I had trouble sleeping at night and functioning at work out of fear for the unknown.

My thoughts drifted towards planning the rest of my days wearing a colostomy bag. What would I eat? Can I still exercise? How often would I need to use the toilet? Is now a good time to take out life insurance?

Luckily the results of genetic testing ruled out the possibility of an FAP. The surgeon scratched his head. "You must be just unlucky."

I felt relieved yet also annoyed he couldn't provide any concreate reason why I have so many polyps.

"Should I change my diet?" I said.

"You can, but no diet will stop your polyps from coming back." he replied.

I remember sadly looking down at the floor. He said the genetic screening only examined a small number of different genes with a potential mutation and the human body has around 20,000.

Interestingly they found I have a condition called Gilbert Syndrome. This is an inherited mutation of the UGT1A1 gene causing difficulties for the liver to properly process bilirubin (break down of red blood cells). It's completely harmless and doesn't require any treatment.

"I need to see you again in twelve months," he said.

Twelve months later I had another colonoscopy with fourteen polyps removed. Although smaller in size, eight of them were still adenomas. I left his office cursing under my breath. It took some time before I accepted the fact I was dodging bullets. Today I'm on a high fiber diet with close surveillance of yearly colonoscopies. At least I now know and can better manage myself. I've come to learn the most dangerous things in life are those we are unaware of or cannot see. Coronavirus is a classic example but this very much includes autism, ADHD and dyslexia. Looking back had I never pushed forward with the bowel screening test I would've found out when my situation was dire. I'm not surprised the recommended bowel screening age has recently dropped to 45 years. According to Bowel Cancer Australia, bowel cancer kills over 5350 Australian's every year, 315 of those younger than age 50.[10]

Things could have been much worse, like what happened to my brother a few years back.

Shocked by going through this experience made me wonder how many others out there have polyps and may not even know. I didn't think telling people would be enough to convince them to go out and buy a bowel screening kit, so I decided to buy a few myself.

I remember smiling and handing one to a girl I was courting on Valentine's Day. She opened the envelope with a wrinkled nose and raised cheeks.

"What the hell is this?" she said.

Our relationship didn't last long. By that stage I'd had so many girls come and go in my life I no longer cared. The way I saw things back then I was saving people's lives. In my eyes I was a hero. My family were much more appreciative of the bowel screening kits. Given our family history of bowel cancer on my dad's side I guess it made more sense.

CHAPTER THIRTY-FIVE

IT WAS A day I'll never forget. From the minute I picked up the phone I knew something was wrong.

Her voice quavered. "Are you the only one home?" she said.

It was my sister-in-law, Luna. I glanced over at skype making sure the microphone was turned off and my friend had signed out. She sounded distressed.

"No one is answering their phone," she said.

"Is something wrong?" I replied.

Luna and my brother had only been married for six months. My first thought was they'd had a fight however it was something far worse. Luna's next words had so much emotion they knocked the complete wind out of me. Struggling to finish her sentence she said, "It's Jack, he's been diagnosed with leukemia."

I remember my body felt like it was caving in, locking into defense mode. Like when a turtle retreats into its shell for protection against predators.

While Luna broke out in tears I fired questions at her like an interrogator. I desperately wanted to know what, when, why and how but she was too upset to answer, and it was still too early to know the full details. The uncertainty left me in a rather unsettled state. I wanted to feel bad for my brother and knew I should be empathizing with Luna or saying something comforting, but I wasn't sure how. As horrible as this sounds, to me hearing about it was like any other surface level conversation, such as talking about the weather or finding out what someone gets up to over the weekend. Obviously, this is clearly unnatural. At the time I wanted to cry with my sister-in-law, but nothing came out. Whacking myself in the head didn't fix the problem either. I remember stammering under my breath, "Just cry god dammit!"

What do you say when you find out your brother has cancer? Back then it was like I needed an instruction manual to tell me what to do and to be honest I'm still not sure now.

My parents and other siblings were also overseas which made the situation more complicated. Luna requested a favor from me to inform them with the horrible news, but I refused.

"I'm a bit busy sorry, I have friends coming over soon," I said.

She ended up having to tell them herself, which she still reminds me about to this day. It was my way of dealing with it. Running away. Looking back now I regret not cancelling my friends' visit but at the time it felt like the only option. Pushing aside my brother's cancer to learn a dance routine with friends allowed me to avoid the problem. And back then I did it surprisingly easy. It was like I didn't fully understand the gravity of the situation. My brother's diagnosis was treated as any other surface level conversation such as the weather. When my friends arrived I was freakishly normal, like nothing had happened. There was no sign of anything strange or any change in my behavior. No one blinked an eyelid. Later on one of the dancers turned down the music when the home phone rang,

"Are you going to answer that?" he said.

I shook my head, knowing very well the call would be about Jack. Straight away it rang a second time, but I refused to answer. Reaching for the power plug it then rung a third time. I scoffed before finally picked up.

Eleanor wailed in misery. "What's happened to mum and dad?"

While holidaying in Bali she received word our parents had abruptly ended their Europe trip and were on the first flight back home. I knew why but wasn't in the mood to talk about it.

"Don't worry," I replied.

My response irritated her. "Tell me!" she said.

"Let's talk about it later, I've got friends over,"

She repeated herself with more volume.

"I'm going to hang up," I said.

With my fingertips on the button she screamed my name with painful force. Saying the words out loud triggered a different response in my brain. It was like a penny had suddenly dropped and the fog was clearing. Hearing about my brother from Luna earlier didn't have much impact but verbalizing it two hours later to my sister over the phone allowed the direness to sink in.

Eleanor immediately left Bali and jumped on the first flight back home. After my friends left I drove straight to the hospital like a hoon, dodging between cars like I had a heavily pregnant lady in the back seat. My heart rate elevated. Looking back now I was lucky not to be pulled over by police.

Arriving with a sense of urgency I said to reception,

"Where's my brother?" I said.

"Slow down sir, what's your brother's name?" the receptionist replied.

She raised her eyebrows with surprise. It appeared Jack was already a celebrity here. The staff knew exactly where to direct me. I stormed into Jack's room in a panic.

"What the fuck is going on, is this some kind of sick joke?" I said.

Jack and his oncologist looked at each other.

"It's ok, he's my brother," Jack said.

I remember hugging Luna and greeting her father thinking, "why is everyone so quiet?" Jack didn't look anxious and was speaking with the doctor in a peaceful manner. I was by far the most agitated person in the room.

After ten minutes of standing up and sitting down from my chair I wanted to leave. I remember walking off around the corner feeling totally bamboozled. Overwhelmed with a variety of intense emotions. Pacing back and forth I couldn't decide whether to stay for my brother's blood test results or go home.

Bang! I began headbutting the wall of Jack's room. Luna's father rested his hand on my shoulder and spoke softly.

"He's going to be ok," he said.

My eyes filled with tears. "I don't understand," I replied.

My behavior here is not too dissimilar from the day at work when I was asked to clean the storeroom. It was evidence of another autistic-related meltdown. Losing control from a tidal wave of stress and overstimulating emotions.

Reflecting on this day it would appear at the beginning I was heartless and didn't care, but as things progressed it was clear I truly did. I just didn't know how to express myself. I felt extremely upset for Jack, it just took longer before I understood and recognized it.

Luna reminds me of comments I made when my brother lost his hair from chemotherapy treatment.

"I can't believe you're still with my brother, I would've just left," I said.

Horrified by my response it wasn't until years later when I realized how inappropriate the comment was. At the time I was simply being honest. Too honest.

Pathological demand avoidance (PDA) and running away from problems are common in those on the spectrum. It is something I've naturally gravitated towards at times when life gets too difficult. After Jack's diagnosis I received a phone call from a bone marrow transplant coordinator. Just the thought of those three words were enough to push me over the edge. Although low, the chances of becoming a donor and going under the knife freaked me out.

I remember waving goodbye to my parents. "I'm going to Africa," I said.

Dad closed his eyes and shook his scruffy mullet. "I wouldn't be doing that, I'll give you the mail,"

Mum looked worried. "What about Ebola?"

I showed them a map of where I was going and where the Ebola virus was, but they weren't at all convinced. Friends from university had invited me to their wedding in South Africa and I needed to get away from the family woes. I hated the emotional seesaw, constantly needing to talk of updates around my brother's cancer every time someone asked how he was doing. I also had trouble navigating others who dodged around the topic. Listening to my parents blame themselves in anguish was also very hard. Waiting around to be guilt tripped into handing out my bone marrow wasn't on the agenda either so leaving the country was a no brainer. I had to go.

However, little did I know at the time I was on the verge of learning another hard lesson. As it turns out the phrase, "when in Rome" does not apply when you're in Africa.

For the record my blood test results confirmed my bone marrow was in fact not a match with Jack. I couldn't be his donor. Bone marrow is the soft spongy tissue inside our bones. It contains our stem cells, the critically important blood cells that produce and develop other blood cells for our immune system. Interestingly Eleanor and I are a match. We share the same genes that code our immune system and stem cells. This was the fascinating commonality I alluded to earlier. Fortunately, my youngest sibling Taylor was the lucky one matching with Jack. At the time of writing there's been no need for any transplant. Hopefully it stays that way.

CHAPTER THIRTY-SIX

SOUTH AFRICA IS not your standard holiday destination. It's a jungle full of human inequality, poverty, racism and disease. It's a dog-eat-dog world with different sets of rules, most of which are not enforced. When hearing stories of racism in the Australian news today I laugh because it's only a tiny fraction of the colorful history in South Africa.

As soon as the novelty of the overseas wedding wore off, I wanted to explore more of Africa. I wanted to see the desert.

"Who wants to come with me?" I said.

None of my friends took me seriously and didn't believe I would actually book flights to Namibia. They were less adventurous and preferred to stick to shopping centers and other common activities such as mini-golf, go-carting and the movies. For me this created a fear of missing out on the good stuff. I had envisaged Africa full of desert and after failing to find any in Cape Town, I was desperate to find some. So much in fact I had forgotten the dangers of my surroundings. Even the security staff at the airport couldn't stop me on my mission. "Where are you staying sir?"

"Near the desert," I replied.

The customs officer peered over the glass then looked down at my passport.

"What tour group are you with?" she said.

I shrugged.

I remember arching back as the customs officer raised her voice. "This is Africa sir! We need to note down where you're going!" Shaking her head in frustration she wrote down "Sossusvlei" on a card then waved me forward.

Sossusvlei is a famous salt and clay pan surrounded by sand dunes in the southern part of the Namib desert. I really wanted to see it however it was a five hour drive from Windhoek airport. By the time I arrived all the tour groups and rental jeeps had been fully booked. There were no last-minute offers or cancellations, which made me nervous.

A taxi pulled up alongside me outside the airport. Looking back now hopping in wasn't the smartest thing to do but at the time it felt like the only option.

Two dark male faces said something in their native language then turned to me in the back seat with a strange look.

"Windhoek?" the driver said.

I smiled and nodded.

Forty-five minutes later the driver dropped me off in an area not too dissimilar from a dusty construction site. I remember swallowing hard, realizing my foolishness when getting out of the taxi. In full view of the loose stones and broken rubble my chest tightened. I pivoted around holes in the pavement while homeless Africans lined the street and gawked with curiosity. It was hard not to gawk back.

One of them pointed to a girl standing inside a tin shed which looked like our family chicken coop back home. A wonky sign labelled, "Imfomation" hung above her head.

"Excuse me, where can I hire a car?" I said.

She gazed up at my red hair with astonishment, then with a

confused look she handed me brochure advertising a politician running for government.

"You vote," she replied.

Rushing down the road I wiped my forehead from fearful sweat. Sweat not just from the humidity but for my life. I had nowhere to go and no one to call for help as my South African sim card no longer had service. Looking back now it was the perfect recipe for disaster.

Aimlessly walking past a café, a man ran out the front door. "Hey! Where are you going bru?" I picked his New Zealand accent straight away which gave me some assurance. He laughed when I told him I wanted to see the desert.

"Only tours go to Sossusvlei bru." he said.

He said I was crazy dragging a case around the streets by myself, especially someone of my appearance. I watched the man hesitantly wave me down another taxi. Stepping back from the road he said,

"Not him he will rob you - that one might stab you… Take this one!"

If he wasn't from New Zealand I wouldn't have trust him.

I was only halfway back to the airport when Jasper, my chirpy taxi driver suddenly pulled over. I gripped the door handle as the car skidded across the sand.

"What are you doing?" I said.

"Do you want to go to Sossusvlei?" he replied.

I rolled my eyes, regretful of bringing it up. "No, not anymore,"

He pulled down his collar showing me a crown logo above his nametag.

"I'm a tour guide!" he said.

I wasn't convinced and remember thinking, "How on earth can a taxi driver be a tour guide."

Desperate to fly back to my friends in South Africa I sighed. "Please just take me to the airport."

But he kept persisting, "I do a good deal."

He licked his lips like he'd stumbled upon a gold nugget, then mumbled something I didn't understand.

While shaking my head his quote increased from $500 to $600 then eventually reached $800. "$800 for everything, $700 if you get food."

I dipped my head and ran my hand through my wet hair. For my own safety I wanted to leave but a small part of me still wanted to visit the Sossusvlei desert. I thought it be a crying shame travelling all this way to Namibia, only to turn around and fly back.

I threw up my hands. "I don't have money to pay you," I said.

Jasper sunk his weathered hand on my knee and smiled. "We go to an ATM," he replied.

Before I had a chance to argue the car was already on the highway heading back to Windhoek. I remember closing my eyes praying under my breath for my safety.

We pulled up in what looked like a McDonalds drive through.

"I know good ATM, it won't rob you," he said.

My chest nervously tightened. Shady locals peered as we stood outside the machine. My driver had his back to me with crossed arms talking to someone in his native tongue.

In this moment I thought if I didn't die here, my bank account will surely get hacked. I remember the machine didn't ask for a PIN number or print out a receipt but surprisingly $800 still came out.

Jasper's face lit up, snatching the cash from my hands then counted it with enthusiasm.

"We go to my home," he said.

"Can we eat first?" I replied. I had the feeling I was in for a rough tour. Unwittingly my life was in his hands.

From the moment he opened his mouth I could tell Jasper was a simple man from limited education. The only topic he knew anything about was money. He had these puffy lips which sprayed saliva during his speech. And he spoke a lot, arguably too much. He also had this ghastly habit I commonly saw among other natives where they'd snort mucus up from their nose then spit it out of their mouths. The sound of it was disgusting. Jasper was also a smoker and I still remember the smell of wretched cigarettes radiating from his clothes. Looking back I don't know how I put up with him for so long.

On our way to his house we passed hundreds of people cooking and eating by the side of the road, washing clothes outside their shanties. I looked out the window at a man dressed in a suit crossing the gravel road. We stopped so he could pass.

"He's going to work," he said.

When we arrived, Jasper instructed me to lay low in the back seat while he spoke to his wife. I watched him step over barbed wire before entering a dwelling, similar to the chicken coop shed I saw earlier. Like every other native African in the country who wasn't a politician or white, he was from a poor upbringing with no opportunities.

I remember waiting in his car thinking if anyone sees me, I'm a goner. There was nowhere to run and I was completely off the grid. After a few minutes his bald head reappeared with a smile. I watched him re-counting the cash. The pile looked much smaller than before.

"We go to eat KFC," he said.

His news brought a moment of joy to me, but when discovering the fast-food store was only a cheap knockoff of the KFC franchise, I became disappointed.

Leaving the city we drove for about three hours down some very dusty roads. There was one point where he told me to hide behind the seat out of fear someone would see my white face and start following us. Finally, we arrived at a secluded roadhouse.

I remember admiring the collusion of sky burst reds and yellows of the sun setting over the flat sand. I was starting to enjoy myself and forget where I was before Jasper upset me. He pointed to the back seat.

Act 2: University and early-career   171

"Goodnight," he said.

My lips pursed. "Wait, we can't both fit in here!"

He argued there wasn't enough money for both of us to stay in the hotel then have enough for the rest of the trip. In my head I knew he'd given half my money away to his wife, but after seeing the Glock 19 in his glovebox I chose to stay quiet. Curled up along a lumpy back seat I punched the door in anger when he left me alone in the car and went inside to his room.

We left early next morning and drove another two hours to the Sossusvlei assembly point. I felt relieved to see two buses full of European tourists. It was the first time I'd seen another white person since leaving the airport. I couldn't wait to explore the salt clay pans and have some time away from Jasper. His repetitive spitting and all the questions about Australia and kangaroos irritated me.

He stayed behind with the locals while I followed the tourist trail.

"I wait here," he said.

The dry landscape scenery was incredible. Here are some photos of me on the white clay pans, surrounded by the 900-year-old dead trees.

After an hour of taking photos and rolling around in the sand

dunes Jasper was nowhere to be seen. I asked one of the locals but he didn't respond. Another shrugged. As the tourists boarded their luxury buses, I remember anxiously pacing back and forth in search for him.

"Do you need a ride?" one of them said.

I panicked. Luckily I had carried a waist bag with the small essentials such as phone, wallet, passport and water but my suitcase holding the rest of my clothes, souvenirs and toiletries was left inside Jasper's car. I couldn't cart it all around the desert with me. My face tensed and I swore under my breath. Suddenly one of the locals approached me from behind.

"He will come back soon, getting fuel," he said.

I wasn't sure whether to believe him, but his friends nodded in agreement and told me to wait.

"How long ago did he leave?" I replied.

From underneath a shady tree I kept my eyes peeled for any movement. Every European tourist had left, and I was all alone in an African desert with a dozen natives who could turn on me at any moment. I was outnumbered and stuck out like a sore thumb. I remember my surroundings being dead still. Scary quiet. The natives didn't even appear to be talking. My mind sifted through all the frightening possibilities of being ganged up, getting eaten by a lion or leopard and passing out from dehydration from the penetrating heat. It's happened before!

Forty-five minutes passed and there were no signs of Jasper. I remember thinking I was going to die. My heart pounded, wondering how on earth I ended up in this situation. If Jasper didn't come back that day, anything could have happened. Then suddenly a faint sound appeared in the distance. It became louder. Once I picked the rattle, I knew it was Jasper's engine. My breathing relaxed however my mood quickly changed from fear to anger.

"Where the hell did you go?" I said.

Looking back on this moment now I can appreciate the reactions of Fatemeh and Jessamine when I did my runner in Las Vegas. Being abandoned is an horrible experience.

Jasper was chewing a bar and answered my question with another question.

"Did you take good pictures?" he said.

He was oblivious to the dangers of the situation. Reflecting on his behaviors now there was a chance he could've also been neurodivergent. Then again maybe the risk at the time wasn't as bad as first thought. Maybe I was freaking out for no reason. We'll never know. Nonetheless he kept me safe and drove me back to the airport in one piece with all my belongings. It was clear Jasper had cleverly taken advantage of my neurodivergent weaknesses and significantly overcharged for his services. He used me as a tool to make a quick buck. Initially this upset me however I'd much rather give away my money to a person living in poverty than a rich person living in luxury.

I remember getting back to South Africa and falling asleep on the couch listening to the waves. A group of us had hired out a beachside mansion in Bloubergstrand with a maid who took care of the household cooking and cleaning.

I opened my eyes to a dark African face poking me with the end of a broom. It took me a few seconds to realize it was the maid.

"Sir!" she said.

"What are you doing?" I replied.

"Are you ok? I thought you were dead," she said.

I laughed but she didn't reciprocate. I wasn't sure if she knew what was funny. It was the middle of the afternoon, and all my friends were still out exploring Cape Town. When I asked her about her day she opened up, sharing flashbacks of her murdered husband on the couch. Apparently this particular day was the anniversary and she thought the same had happened to me. I wasn't sure what to say so I pointed to my head and made a joke.

"Did he have red hair too?" I said.

She sighed, dropping her pointy chin and swept the floor. I

wanted to cheer her up so I jumped off the couch and offered her a hug. She stopped and looked at me with hesitation.

"You are a funny man," she said.

Whether it was her broken English, dark African skin or musty smell it sparked an idea. One which I've been told many wouldn't ever dare try.

When she let go of my body I refused to release from the hug. She looked up into my eyes with confusion.

I smiled. "Have you ever kissed a white man?" I said.

She gasped with astonishment then shook her head.

"We not allowed to sir," she replied.

I remember wanting to respond with an apartheid joke but instead leaned forward with pouted lips. She didn't hold back for a good two minutes. It was another happy ending to a treacherous overseas trip. But unlike my previous romance in Sri Lanka, the African maid seemed to want more. Her pupils dilated.

"I love you!" she said.

I stepped back and squinted. "You love me already?"

She nodded with intensity, "Yes, take me with you."

"Where are we going?" I replied.

At the time I was blown away by her extreme level of desperation. It reminded me of ruthlessly wanting to know the results of my genetic screening.

"Um, I'm not sure you'll fit inside my suitcase," I replied.

My Australian friends from this trip still cry with laughter when I retell this story. They also share other cringeworthy moments of my behavior, one of which I ask the bride to drive us home at the end of her wedding night because I wasn't sober enough. Thankfully she did get us home safely and still talks to me today.

All this happened when I was twenty-seven. I was a tertiary educated adult, brought up in a stable family who arguably made not one, not two but a collection of dicey decisions. Most people can't imagine experiencing anything like this over their entire lifetime. Back then I didn't think much of it and assumed it was just part of my unlucky (or lucky?) world. Today I'm grateful I'm still alive to share these stories. It's amazing where life can take you when the compass inside your head functions differently to everyone else.

CHAPTER THIRTY-SEVEN

HERE'S ANOTHER JAW-DROPPING story from my collection of dicey-decisions. One time my best friend Kiel gave me the keys to his apartment so I could use his shower. At the time our shower was off-limits when my family were renovating. He lived on the ground floor inside a group of high-rise apartment buildings around the city. It was a nice spot with access to a gym and swimming pool. Kiel was an only child and well looked after by his parents. Although he'd never say it, I know he didn't buy the apartment all by himself. From the early years in primary school I'd hear about all the Christmas gifts he'd receive from his parents and relatives. Generous items such as PlayStation sets, remote control cars, cubby houses and even basketball rings mounted in the backyard. His parents went to a lot of trouble. I remember growing up I'd invite myself over just so I could play his latest version of Duke Nukem on his computer. He had all the latest games. Sometimes I'd get envious and complain to dad why Santa couldn't bring me any of these things. His reply was always, "That boy is kissed on the dick by a fairy!"

For a while I thought he was talking about the tooth fairy and sometimes went to bed without wearing my pants hoping I'd get lucky.

As mentioned earlier Kiel was my best mate fortunate to go to a prosperous private school. The school I wanted to transfer to from Egan High. I'm sure he had his own demons but through my eyes (or compared to me anyway) he appeared to have life easy.

After first meeting in kindergarten we were tied at the hip sitting next to one another every year of primary school. Once we were separated at high school we lost touch for a while however because our parents were close, Kiel has stayed in the picture. And thankfully so because through thick and thin he has always stuck by my side and been the most loyal of mates. The perfect choice for a best man!

I'd visited Kiel's apartment before. The building had a blue tinge on all the windows which mirrored your reflection. I'd usually see a gardener floating around pulling out weeds and trimming hedges, even though he didn't need to. The place looked immaculate. With a towel over my shoulder, I ventured over on a weekday when he was at work. Swiping his security tag against the sensor, for some unknown reason the door wouldn't open for me. Even after several attempts turning it over, holding it upside down in different positions, the light was flashing red.

"It's not working?" one of the residents said.

I shook my head before the man swiped his tag. The door opened straight away. At the time I thought it was odd but didn't dwell for long. Heading inside I inserted the key into the front door of Kiel's apartment, 24A. I remember never actually feeling the unlocking mechanism of the door which made me question whether the door was already unlocked. It was hard to know for sure. I messaged Kiel, "Did you lock your front door this morning?" Nevertheless, when the door opened and I saw the layout which was exactly how I remembered it from last time. As you enter the front door, the kitchen is up ahead on the left and the bathroom on the immediate right. Reaching for the light switch I messaged Kiel again, "Hey, you left your kitchen light on silly!"

Over the next half hour I had used the toilet, had a shower and washed my hair with Kiel's shampoo and conditioner. Before leaving I also left a small box of chocolates on his kitchen bench as a way of saying thank you.

On my way home Kiel called me during his lunch break.

"Were the lights really on and the door unlocked?" he said.

He thought I was playing a trick on him. We laughed, ending our short conversation under the assumption the careless boy must have forgotten. It's the sort of thing I forget too!

Two days later I returned to the apartment for another shower. Retracing my steps I suddenly felt a case of Deja-vu. The same door refused to open. Looking around I remember checking to make sure there was nowhere else to swipe and no other access points. Nothing. The light continued to flash red. What was I missing? After a few minutes of waiting suddenly the door opened when someone inside was coming out. It is here I wish I'd turned around and gone home but curiosity well and truly had the better of me that day. I was laser focused on having a shower and nothing could stop me.

I arrived at apartment 24A and checked the door handle. Kiel's door was unlocked. At the time I thought it was strange but given the same thing happened two days earlier, I gave Kiel benefit of the doubt. For all I knew there could've been a problem with his front door and/or his extra security tag.

Only there wasn't. Behind my back were a family sitting on their couch studying me very carefully. I remember pulling the towel from around my neck and reaching for the bathroom. It was a few seconds before my peripheral vision kicked in. My body froze in shock like a statue. I then turned and looked down at the toddler eating the chocolates I had left behind two days earlier. Kiel was single and certainly didn't have kids. He was also Caucasian and the toddler looked Latino. The parents stood up from the couch waiting in fear for me to speak or at least explain what on earth I was doing. My mouth opened to say something, but nothing came out except for air.

I then covered my mouth with a hand while a voice inside my head yelled, "Holy shit what have I done!". The penny finally dropped. This was not Kiel's apartment at all. I had been showering in this family's apartment by mistake.

"Who are you?" the father said.

I mumbled in a panic. "Oh sorry, wrong shower!"

Before he had a chance to question me any further I quickly U turned and ran out the door faster than Usain Bolt. It turned out Kiel's apartment, 24A was in fact in the building next door. I had the correct apartment number, correct floor but the wrong building. In my defense all the buildings look the same!

Kiel has never let me get away with this and still brings it up regularly. When I share this story some people say they would've likely made the same mistake, which may be true but looking back the warning signs were there, and I failed to see them. It just didn't register. What happened here falls under the same umbrella as all the other funny and wild adventures I've been dragged into by my undiagnosed conditions.

CHAPTER THIRTY-EIGHT

THE ART OF holding back and thinking before acting is a skill most people develop with maturity into adulthood. Everyone makes mistakes sometimes however by a certain age there's a level of expectation, a.k.a. age-appropriate behavior. For most of my life this expectation has felt out of reach and the only way around it is by masking or camouflaging. This is hiding or disguising parts of my authentic self to better fit in and connect with others. I've come to learn this is one of the most fascinating aspects around autism. And like many others on the spectrum I didn't even realize I was doing it. It seamlessly melded into what I thought was normal reality. As I've read from expert sources, masking is like a secret identity woven into the fabric of one's existence, hiding one's true self beneath layers of social adaption.

When to mask and how much is also a challenge because every situation has a completely different set of circumstances. For example who am I in the presence of? Is this a first encounter? Have I known the person(s) a long time and have they ever seen me out of my shell? Who else might they tell? Repeating lines back exactly the way others have said them (echolalia) is also a good trick. So is scripting and rehearsing future conversations. On many occasions

I've also nodded in agreeance and said things like, "Yes I know" and "Oh really?" pretending to side with people. This happens when I don't or sometimes can't listen properly because my brain is still processing something else. It also happens when I listen but don't understand someone's point of view or share the same feelings. For me masking is in full mode when in professional environments at work. It usually performs well but there have been times my true personality overpowers and shines through.

I remember one time detouring from the bar when Kiel tapped me on the chest. "I need to ask you something." His fiancé peeped over his shoulder. I got ready to take their drink order.

"I want you to be my best man," he said.

My jaw dropped. Then like a rotating clown head at a carnival I looked around the busy venue unable to speak. I was extremely overwhelmed and caught off-guard. How do you respond to something like that? I wasn't sure whether to go with a powerful, "oh my god that's so exciting!" keep it formal, "Thank you mate." or respond in question, "Are you serious?" All of these can be said in different ways to express different meanings. The options for me that night were endless. I remember they both laughed as the window of time to respond had lapsed. Out of respect for my best mate I desperately needed to do something, so I touched my forehead with the back of my hand then made a fainting sound.

Their laughter intensified when I collapsed on the floor. Turning the conversation into a game of charades I had communicated (hopefully) to them, "Yes, I'd be honored,"

Little did I know the demands of being his best man would exceed my sensory limits. The night before his wedding things got out of control. We were out drinking with the bridal party and some of Kiel's relatives at a local bar. I stood in a circle with the other groomsman, talking of the big day ahead. I remember one of them was rather annoying and seemed to enjoy hitting people in the groin, particularly me.

"Stop!" I said.

The groomsman laughed when he missed my genitals by a whisker. I pressed my lips together, on guard to block his next hit. One of the others egged him on. They were all from Kiel's school and at the time it felt like deja vu, standing in harm's way of another bully feeding off the enjoyment from his followers. Ironically this groomsman had a pointy nose similar to that of Scott Read.

Once he started removing my hat and throwing it away, it got under my skin. Feeling the temperature rise inside my body I remember thinking if he tries doing it again, I'm going to react.

With an angry look on my face I told him to stop. Seconds later he leaned forward holding his fist with a mischievous grin. Looking back now it is here I should've turned around and walked away instead of choosing the wrong path.

Squeezing my glass of cider in bubbling fury, I flung it forward with aggression. Seconds later he whined from the sting. I remember my attention was immediately drawn to the table of distressed outsiders wiping their clothes.

"I'm so sorry," I said.

Following the collateral damage to the bar I offered to buy him a jug of beer which appeared to calm him down. On my return the doused groomsman was still rubbing his eyes from the cider. I chuckled to myself and didn't feel the need to apologize. The scene was like a repeat of the high school drama where my retaliation felt valid. In my eyes he deserved it, but just like Scott and Bart this groomsman didn't seem to agree. Gripping onto my collar his red eyes illuminated in my face.

"Let's take this outside," he said.

While being dragged out of the venue I remember thinking why? Didn't he understand he was being a jerk. Standing over me he stabbed his fingers into my sternum,

"You don't deserve to be the best man!" he said.

I hated every time I tried to speak, he spoke over the top, protesting against my childish behavior, lack of involvement in the groom and pre-wedding festivities. Squirming from the chest ache I clenched my fists preparing to throw a punch. I'd never punched someone before so I wasn't exactly sure how to do it. While he ranted in my face, I thought about what hand to use, where exactly to hit him and how hard. Luckily Kiel broke us up before I finalized my decision.

"Hey!" he said.

Bolting down the road I left them behind to talk things out. Crunching into a ball I camouflaged myself amongst the greenery. I remember hearing Kiel call out my name but I didn't respond. I wanted to be left alone. I needed time to calm down and process all my thoughts and emotions from the confrontation.

At the time I had no idea what Kiel's groomsman was rambling on about and why. Everything he accused me of was false. Previously I had organized Kiel's bucks party, helped decorate and setup the wedding venue as well as taken care of the ring. It didn't make sense.

A few hours later we were forced to shake hands and make amends however things still didn't feel right on the day. I remember avoiding him wherever possible. More importantly the wedding was still a success and Kiel thoroughly enjoyed his special day.

There was one special moment though which will go down in history. As I stood beside him Kiel projected his wedding vows into the microphone for the celebrant. All eyes of the 150 guests were glued to the five of us on the stage. His soon to be wife and maid of honor included.

"Bless, O Lord, the giving of these rings, so that they who wear them may abide in peace and continue in thy favour," the celebrant said.

Kiel nudged my hip. It was my time to shine. Reaching deep into my pocket I pulled out a brown ring box. I remember the box was made from a furry fabric which made my fingertips tingle.

Looking back now I blame the uncomfortable fabric for not knowing I was holding the box upside down. With the entire venue waiting for me to hand over the wedding ring, I turned my body towards Kiel and opened the box at the same time. Due to forces of gravity the ring was hanging loose inside, then frightfully spilled out, falling towards the ground. In a deep panic my shoulders raised up into my neck and my chest tightened with extreme fear. Time ticked over in slow motion as the ring continued to fall. I remember hearing a gasp from the front row before an odd applause. Kiel's left hand had suddenly appeared out of nowhere and caught the ring before it hit the ground. It was indeed an amazing recovery and a show stopping performance.

Shortly after I was hovering around with shameful red cheeks believing I'd just ruined the best day of Kiel's life. But it turned out quite the opposite. Everyone was impressed.

"So how did you pull off the ring trick? Was it tied to a string?" someone said.

Kiel certainly doesn't have any regrets so I guess I shouldn't be too worried about it either. We still joke about it to this day. A few years later I also reached out to the groomsman to apologize for the cider incident. It was received very well. One thing I've learned in life is it's never too late to apologize.

CHAPTER THIRTY-NINE

HOW DO YOU know when you've found the right partner? This was a question I asked Kiel after his wedding.

"You just know," he said.

I stood there dumbfounded. "But how?" I replied.

At the time I thought Chaturi might be the right one for me. Main reason being she hung around much longer than all the others. We had been on and off for over 2 years and enjoyed each other's company. I would visit her after breakdancing classes and she'd spoon-feed me juicy pomegranate seeds. She was invited to join me at Kiel's wedding, but sadly we broke up the week prior. Reflecting on things now, I had great difficulty understanding her sarcasm and being emotionally available when she needed me the most. Two common areas of weakness for those on the spectrum.

I've come to learn finding the right partner requires a deep level of intuition as well as metacognition, which is an awareness and understanding of one's own thought processes. This skill helps a person recognize how they feel about another person. It allows someone to choose the right career for their own interests and talents. It also steers you when buying or selling a house, deciding whether or not to become a parent and how to manage your finances. An internal compass. Unlike my neurodivergent self, neurotypical Kiel could do this seamlessly, making big decisions with a low margin of error.

My dating life followed a similar trend to my career choices. Unpredictable, experimental and error prone. As I look down at the keloid scar next to my belly button, I recall one of the first dates I ever went on with a girl.

I had invited Rita around to the house for a study session while my parents were away. We met each other in a developmental biology class at university. Like most of the girls I was drawn to she was dark. Not quite as dark as Imani but from the same part of the world.

In the lead up to her arrival I became increasingly nervous and excited, feeling the need to impress her. I remember vacuuming the house, wiping the kitchen and setting up a comfortable area for us with beanbags and scented candles. I even bleach cleaned and deodorized the toilet which is something I never do. My phone vibrated. "Here!" she messaged.

I looked out the window but couldn't see her car. Our house had a steep and long graveled driveway running some 80 meters. She had parked at the bottom not realizing there was space at the top. In hindsight I should've messaged her to drive up however I was far too excited to wait any longer to see her. Like coyote chasing after roadrunner, I sprinted down our driveway oblivious to the uneven surfaces. Over time rainwater had created many hazardous potholes and trenches. The first time mum fell over and grazed her arm, dad was supposed to have the driveway repaired. Nearly a decade past before he did anything.

"There's a bloke at the club with a bobcat, I will call him next week," he'd say.

I remember the moment my foot got caught something awful was about to happen. Due to the overload of enthusiastic downward force my body suddenly projectiled through the air and headed for a pine-tree. I put up my hands to break the fall, but it didn't stop the razor sharp branch slicing my skin. Rita was greeted by a wounded soldier wearing a blood-stained shirt. It immediately ruined any chances of romance.

She pointed to my stomach. "Oh my god! Are you ok?" she said.

Once the floaters in my eyes and dizziness faded we went inside. I remember she wiped clean my stomach then offered to take me to hospital.

"I think you need stitches," she said.

I refused, trying to act tough through the painful sting. I regret this decision now. Had I've gone to hospital that day the keloid scar would only be a fraction of the size it is today.

Since I was unfit to study and not interested in seeing a doctor, Rita decided to cut her visit short. I asked her to stay but she wanted to let me rest. After that the window of opportunity was closed. Our friendship was reduced back to normal, and we only occasionally bumped into one another around the university campus.

Rita is one of many girls throughout my twenties I have tried to score points with but finish up receiving a red card. I remember a petite Asian girl I was keen on one time. She was kind enough to drive me all the way home after a late night in the city. We arrived at the top of our driveway around 2am. Before hopping out I leaned in for a kiss. She smiled and leaned in too. However before we had a chance to close our eyes, the car interior suddenly lit up with a warm glow. Someone had turned on the balcony lights outside. It wasn't long before dad's voice penetrated through the windows. "Hey Trav!"

I remember she scorned with surprise. "Who's that man?" she said.

I turned around to see dad standing there in his nighttime underwear and unkept grey mullet. Like a creepy homeless person he squinted at the car while scratching at the psoriasis on his beer belly.

"Have you got my train ticket?" he said.

Closing my eyes and pinching my nose, I sighed. My poor date looked mortified. The excitement inside the car vanished. Earlier that day I'd borrowed my dad's yearly train ticket to save some money getting into the city. For some reason he couldn't sleep until it was back in his wallet. I'm not sure why. He didn't pay for it. He'd found it on the ground one day when walking to the train station. Once dad started moving towards the car she turned on the engine, making it clear she wanted to leave.

"Thanks so much again for the lift," I said.

She drove off in a hurry. Still half asleep, my dad stared at her car until it was completely out of sight.

"Who was that?" he said.

Hands on hips I shook my head. I remember messaging her again the next day but didn't get a response. Dad had scared her away.

Interestingly something else which has created hardship for me on the dating scene are my hypersensitivities. Whether it be light, sound, touch or taste there have been times when I would overreact and even sometimes freak out to an overload of sensory stimulation. It's a common experience for those on the spectrum to have heightened sensitivities to sensory stimuli. Of course, back in my twenties I had no idea what this was.

I've already alluded to my first blue light disco. It turns out scuba diving causes similar problems for me. An African American girl I was dating for a while happened to be an experienced diver.

I'd first met Shanice on the Brooklyn bridge in New York during my mid-semester holiday break. We kept in contact over social media before she decided to visit me a few months later. I remember the extreme excitement and nervousness picking her up from Sydney airport. I'd made a personalized "Welcome to Australia" sign decorated with kangaroos, koalas and our national flag.

She lived in Harlem and worked with popular artists in the music industry. With a background in singing she had this soothing voice with a thick American accent which lured me in. She spoke in a soft range singers refer to as thin folds. Listening to her would sometimes trigger a static-like or tingling sensation on the skin around my scalp which then moved down the back of my neck. I loved it because it always calmed me down and at times felt as though my body was drifting off to sleep. I'd had similar experiences before with Nethu in Sri Lanka and even when listening to certain teachers in school. I've come to learn this is called autonomous sensory meridian response (ASMR) and happens in around 20% of people (both neurodivergent and neurotypical). The most relatable experience I can compare it to is the anxiety relief music you hear at massage parlors and beachside resorts.

"Hey boo, would you like to go diving?" Shanice said.

I nodded multiple times. I had no idea what scuba diving actually involved, but the thought of seeing her busty figure in bathers was too hard to resist. A week later we were sliding on our wetsuits, oxygen masks, goggles, and flippers with a group of 10 strangers inside an aquarium. To my dismay I couldn't see much through the foggy eyewear. I also didn't enjoy breathing through a tube which tasted like rubber. My experience only sunk further once I entered the water tank. Everyone in the group quickly picked up the basic skills and were able to stay under the water, except me.

Shanice lowered her goggles. "Is something wrong?" she said.

"I can't breathe under the water," I replied.

"Is your oxygen working?"

I sighed. "Yeah."

The instructor was also getting frustrated and had given up on me. For some reason every time I tried to stay under the water my body would seize with sheer panic. A flight or fright response would kick in rapidly increasing my breathing and heart rate, leaving no choice but for me to rise to the surface. It was like my brain couldn't fathom the concept of being able to breath under water using the equipment. I watched the group swim off into the deep blue water.

"Come on, quit bugging me out!" Shanice said.

I shook my head with apprehension. She grabbed my hands and gently pulled me under the water. I squeezed as my breathing rate skyrocketed again like I was running a marathon. After a minute of desperately forcing myself to stay, I couldn't bare another second. It was just too uncomfortable. Embarrassingly I left the water and headed for the change rooms, waiting for Shanice and the group to return. Later on I asked the reception for a refund, but they refused saying my reasons were outside their returns policy. I also apologized to Shanice hoping it might smooth things over but she still looked deflated. For the rest of the trip things seemed ok however not long after flying back, she posted a picture of herself with a new boyfriend. I tried to stay in contact, but it was clear from the no responses she had lost interest.

Another agonizing hypersensitivity giving me grief is something most girls have a lot of. Hair. When fine strands of hair touch my skin, it can be incredibly irritating. Similar to a reflex action after being tickled or bitten by a mosquito, it's made intimacy with girls extra complicated. I'll never forget one time I was lucky enough to be invited back to a girl's bedroom. We met on one of those Contiki tours overseas where you're constantly inundated with alcohol.

Her name was Julia, and she was an overly tall blonde from the Netherlands. Given her fair complexion I wasn't interested at first. But as the tour continued I felt sorry for her when seeing many of the guys rudely turn her down. I also overheard some of them joke about her height. She was well over 6 foot and taller than nearly everyone. I've never understood the sin behind dating a girl who's taller than you. If anything it should be the opposite. For a straight guy, finding a girl is like winning a trophy. The taller the girl, the bigger the trophy.

On one of the last nights I noticed Julia sitting by herself on her phone. Her friends were too occupied with other guys, so I went over to keep her company.

"Cool phone," I said.

She gave me a surprised look then smiled. Her mouth moved but the music inside the venue was so loud I couldn't hear what she was saying. After finishing our drinks we walked back to our hotel rooms which were conveniently located across the road from the venue. I remember we linked arms to prevent us from stumbling.

Julia invited me inside her room. I yawned, thinking nothing of it however once the door closed, she became quite aroused. Next thing I remember I was lying face down on her bed. My drowsiness quickly turned into excitement as Julia jumped on top of me and pulled off my shirt like a Band-Aid.

"Turn over!" she said aggressively.

I looked up at her in a trance. She arched back and removed her hair ties, allowing full extension of her floppy blonde locks. Her hair then landed onto my naked abdomen with heavy force. I clenched my fists and curled my toes while she kissed areas around my belly button. I cringed with extreme discomfort. Her lips felt like laying on a dreamy pillow, but her hair felt like rusty nails scraping on tempered glass.

I remember doing sit-ups, trying to grab and lift it off my skin. It didn't appear to phase Julia. Her lips kept moving lower. But before she had a chance to remove my underwear, I pulled out.

"Stop!" I said.

Julia sat up and narrowed her eyes. "What's wrong? Are you gay?"

Looking back on this moment now I wish I had asked her to put her hair ties back on. It would have saved us the awkward conversation. At the time I couldn't understand or even begin to explain what I was experiencing. I nodded, even though deep down I didn't believe I was actually gay. This is one example of masking, allowing me to escape without hurting Julia's feelings.

CHAPTER FORTY

ONCE UPON A time I'd look back at all the episodes in my life and think why? Why do I seem to attract misfortune? Why do I tend to experience bad things and need to learn from them the hard way? Am I just unlucky like my colorectal surgeon said or are other forces at play? Of course, there are plenty of people out there worse off but most have a reason or at the very least know why. In Australia one knows if they live in poverty, have a drug addiction, have been brought up in an abusive family or missing a limb. They have an explanation for their misfortune and can (if they choose to) put the right steps in place, working towards improvement. Back then I didn't even know where to start. At times my situation felt helpless, and I'd think either I'm cursed or doomed for failure. The world around me felt dangerous and the only obvious way to be safe was to stop trying to fit into society, run away and live a life in solitude. Many times, I've considered to take this easy way out, but knew deep down it wouldn't achieve anything. The only option making sense was to stay resilient and keep moving forward in the hope one day my life will get better. One day the stairway will lead me to a life of enjoyment and success.

And that's when I met her. She was assigned to look after me in hospital after one of my colonoscopy procedures. Her name was

Dakanda Wattanajinda. She was a nurse from Thailand and had only been in Australia for a short time on a student/working visa. I remember the first thing which struck me about her were her almond eyes. Naturally I've always shied away from eye contact with girls but when she entered my field of view, I couldn't stop myself from looking. Her eyes had this alluring Asian persuasion of a Brown Iris underneath long lashes. She had this infectious smile which lit up my room, making me forget about my stomach pains. She was also kind-hearted and served me extra sandwiches whenever I requested more food. On occasions when she'd ask me how I was feeling I'd always respond with uncertainty, forcing an investigation from her so she'd have to stay around longer. Within the first couple of interactions with her I could tell she was shy and introverted, but her English skills were good enough to laugh at all my bad jokes.

After I was discharged, I didn't believe I would ever see her again. But my disappointment was short lived because the following day I noticed her social media profile appear under my suggested friends. My heart skipped a beat with excitement. They say our phone technology listens to us and can pick up on our daily interactions. It's both extremely concerning and miraculous!

"Hey, I owe you a sandwich! When can we meetup again?" I wrote via messenger. According to the app, she'd seen my message but didn't reply. "Let's make it two sandwiches!" I wrote. Again, still no reply but could see she had viewed my messages. After a few days I decided to get more creative. "I'm ordering your sandwiches from Bangkok and will deliver them to you on one bended knee!" I wrote again, even including a photoshopped picture of me bending down in action. This time I finally heard a response.

"Hey! How are you? You are a funny man. Ok, when do you want to meet?" she replied.

Over the following weeks Dakanda and I met up a few times over coffee. I was fascinated learning about her family and the ways governments operate in her country. Compared to my standard Australian upbringing it seemed much more interesting.

Dakanda was the youngest of four children, all of which had left home and settled in other countries. Her parents along with her army of 42 close relatives still lived in Thailand, around the affluent suburbs of Bangkok. Her father was a doctor who spent generous time caring for impoverished villages and her mother was a lawyer, both of which Dakanda said pressured her into following similar career paths. It was apparently one of the main reasons she had chosen to come to Australia. Most of her family relatives were well educated and had good jobs in medicine, law, business or the government. One of her sisters was a professional soccer player and had represented Thailand in the Olympics. I was blown away to hear her sister had even scored a goal against Brazil in their first qualifying match. Sadly the team missed out on making it through to the final round.

Interestingly her grandmother was one of the oldest living citizens in Thailand. At the staggering age of 103 she was well recognized by the public and still fit enough to parade down the streets for their Chinese New Year celebrations.

The Wattanajinda family were also strong supporters of the Catholic faith, which was rare in Thailand as most of the population were Buddhist. Dakanda shared stories about their weekly Sunday sessions at church and daily prayers at the dinner table. I remember watching her during our dates raise her right hand over her forehead, chest and shoulders chanting, "Bless us, O Lord, and these, Thy gifts, which we are about to receive from Thy bounty. Through Christ, our Lord. Amen."

One time I pulled a Bounty chocolate bar from my pocket and took a bite after she'd finished.

"Yes, thank you bounty," I said.

She found it hilarious. Without breaking a sweat, Dakanda was ticking boxes I never knew existed. Before meeting her I'd only ever heard of these things from the movies. Never had I come into contact with anyone who was related to or let alone actually knew a professional soccer player and a centenarian. Religion was also a foreign language to me.

All of my grandparents were well and truly resting in peace, two of which passed away in their 50's from heart failure. I'd never even met them! My mum dropped out of high school in form 3 and had worked across different administration jobs. Dad barely scraped through school. In his senior years he'd started a fire by igniting fireworks inside the school recycling bins. He was lucky not to be expelled. Nonetheless he still ended up with a decent job designing maps for the mining industry.

Comparatively Dakanda's family sounded higher up the food chain but what admired me was the way she spoke about them. She appeared genuinely proud of their achievements and not at all envious or boastful. She didn't rub it in my face or see me as inferior, which is often the case I see in movies.

As the months continued, I became more and more surprised Dakanda hadn't yet run away. Based on my dating history it was expected to happen at any moment. But the day never came. I introduced her to my family as well as Kiel, Peter and Allan, all of which she gained their respect. Family was at the heart of her culture.

I remember Dakanda pulling me aside at my parents' house.

"I can't understand your dad," she said.

I laughed. This didn't surprise me. Dad would megaphone Aussie questions and phrases at her in his thick bogan accent. He also had a long list of similes and metaphors in his vocabulary.

"How are you champ? Are you winning? Do you want a beer? Let me know if you need to use the little house on the prairie."

At times I got the feeling he was intentionally making it harder for Dakanda, capitalizing on her limited understanding of Australian slang.

"Mate, she's a lovely girl, I just hope she's allowed to stay," Dad said.

It turned out Dad's question happened to be on everyone's mind. Except for my own. Dakanda gave regular updates on her visa paperwork, but I never took it seriously. As selfish as this may sound, unless a situation affects me deeply on personal level, it's hard for my autistic brain to justify giving it much attention or thought. This is arguably the main reason why I've failed in so many romantic relationships.

Her expiry date loomed and Dakanda became quite distressed. She gripped my body tight like an authority was trying to drag her away.

"What's going to happen if I need to leave?" she said.

The topic also sparked interest from family members which apparently, they'd all been gossiping about. Dad sat me down one day and gave me a stern look. "Look son, don't do anything stupid alright. I watch the channel seven news."

I stared blankly back at him, clueless on what he was talking about. El and her boyfriend kept poking fun repeatedly asking me, "What's the going rate?"

"$11.50/hour," I'd say, not knowing the underlining meaning behind their question. I finally found out later on they believed I was getting paid by Dakanda's family to commit to dating her and take her hand in marriage. It sounds absurd but apparently it was a common conspiracy in Australia at the time to smuggle people into the country.

It wasn't until a work colleague warned me of the potential risks did I fully understand what I might be up against. His brother had married a Thai girl, allowing her to stay in Australia and apply for permanent residency (a green card). Only a few months into the marriage he discovered his wife was transferring money from their joint bank account back home to her family. Then after several arguments around it she later divorced him and ran away with half of his assets.

Murky feelings rumbled in my stomach and I remember avoiding Dakanda for a few days while digesting all the feedback. Even though I really liked Dakanda, there was a possibility she might one day rob me. And there was also a possibility her family might offer to pay me to marry her. And then Dakanda might decide to rob me later on. At first I was scared but then I shook my head because none of it made sense. Not only was Dakanda a kindhearted soul but there was no reason for her to rob me. She didn't need to. At the time I was drowning in financial university debt and from what I gathered the Wattanajinda family were already successful. Dakanda's parents could afford to fund her expensive education fees which allowed her to stay in the country.

After pondering over this for a few days I decided to put myself out of misery. Looking back now it was the first time in my life I had a chance to avoid harm's way before it found me first.

CHAPTER FORTY-ONE

I PICKED DAKANDA up from work one afternoon and took her for a stroll in the park. I remember it being a hot summer day, the sun penetrating thick layers of sunscreen over my white skin.

Dakanda voiced a concern. "Why didn't you message me this week?" she said.

I rolled my eyes, hearing the question from her many times before. Regrettably I have a reputation of sending delayed responses or even sometimes failing to acknowledge or reply back to a message. Not because I don't care, but rather simply forget or not know what to write. It was a communication problem I had with many people, not just her. A common symptom for the neurodivergent community. In saying that for me writing a message is far easier than speaking because there's more time to consider your words. It also removes any chance of stuttering. There have been many times when speaking to people I need to omit and replace words last minute for fear I won't be able to say the word fluently. Or they'll be something I'm trying to say but the word which comes out has a different meaning. It's incredibly frustrating. I've noticed it's worse at loud venues and places with lots of background noise like bars and sporting events etc. Ironically alcohol seems to improve things. Maybe this is why people drink.

At the time I had a reason for being distant with Dakanda.

"I need to ask you something. It's very important," I said.

Dakanda gasped. "What is it?" she replied.

"Yang," I said, which is her native tongue for "not yet". I'd been practicing some small words from the Thai language. Sitting underneath a shady tree, I opened up with sharpness.

"Are you going rob me?" I said.

Dakanda quickly rebutted, "What?"

I paused, thinking of a better way to say it.

"Are you planning to rob me one day?" I said in a softer tone.

Dakanda's face blushed into an awkward red. "What are you talking about?" she said.

I suspiciously looked her up and down, then after a few seconds finally realized she had no idea what I was talking about. After I filled her in on the conversations I'd had with family and friends, a tear ran down her cheek.

"Do you believe that?" she said.

I looked down and shrugged. She raised the volume.

"You are so fucking stupid!" she said.

I remember holding myself back from laughing at her high-pitched voice. The way she cursed the F word was so cute.

"I would never do that to you! I don't need to! I am a skilled worker!" she said.

I looked up at the birds retreating from their branches to escape the unwanted noise. Dakanda then stood up with conviction.

"I am not poor, and I'm lucky I can borrow money from my parents to pay for education here!" she said.

I remember thinking inside my head, "I wish I could say that." At the time my education debt was (and still is!) accumulating with indexation fees. Listening to the hurt in her voice, it became clear everyone, including myself had very wrongly misjudged her. I felt like an idiot that day. Looking back at this now I kick myself for being so foolish. The conversation changed course, revealing a list of bad things Dakanda thought about our relationship. Some of them gave me deja vu from previous relationships. Over the year we were together she believed:

- I treated her more as a friend and not a girlfriend.
- There was not enough intimacy, affection or romance from my end. i.e. Regular hugs and kisses both physical and via phone.
- I didn't prioritize her or plan enough to organize dates, even when celebrating special occasions like her birthday.
- We lacked understanding where she needed to repeat herself and explain things to me multiple times.
- I was forgetful and often failed to listen/pay attention to things she said.
- I rarely expressed myself which left her feeling emotionally empty. i.e. She never heard me say the magical three words, "I love you" and genuinely mean it.

Dakanda picked up her bag in a huff. "I'm done!" she said.

I remember sitting on the ground with crossed legs, watching her storm off towards the train station. At the time I didn't entirely agree with her point of view however her last point hit me like a tonne of bricks because I knew it was true. She had already verbalized and messaged the words, "I love you" to me a few times before and I didn't know how to take it. Seeing how it's done in movies I knew the words needed to be relayed back but as bad as this sounds, I wasn't sure if I truly loved her or not. How does one actually know? Is there some kind of formula? Again I think it's one of those deeper intuition things most people like Kiel do without much effort.

The full brink around our conversation in the park didn't hit me until a few days later. It was then I realized I didn't want to break up with her. She was too good to let go. I'd never met another girl before who could put up with my personality, poor cooking skills, sweaty clothes, survive a conversation with my dad, offer to clean my ears and take days off work to look after me when feeling ill.

After persistently calling her and then driving past with a colorful array of flowers, a few of weeks later we were back on good terms. To my surprise Dakanda also apologized for her behavior in the park. She explained she'd had a rough day at work and was looking after a difficult patient, fueling her foul mood. I'd seen her mood swings before but my foolishness in the park that day bolstered it to another level. Once Dakanda and I started dating again, she threw a curveball at me.

"Come to Thailand with me, my parents want to meet you!" she said.

I swallowed hard. "Oh ok, really, do they?"

She saw the apprehension in my face then questioned why I wouldn't jump at the opportunity.

"I would like to meet them, but I just need to think about it, it's a big commitment," I said.

The thought of travelling overseas again was exciting but knew this trip would be different. It would either make or break our relationship. Looking back now it felt like an ultimatum. Visiting Thailand would keep us alive but staying in Australia risked losing Dakanda for good. Luckily, I decided to book the airfare.

From what I knew about Dakanda's parents, they sounded quite different to mine. Opinionated, disciplinary and traditional with strong values and beliefs. They had rather high expectations for their children which made me nervous thinking they'd have even higher expectations for me. She reassured me though her parents would accept me because I was kind and gentle. Dakanda shared a story with me when her parents refused to engage with her brother after he was caught in his bedroom with a girl he'd brought home one night.

I guess it was no surprise I was asked to book a hotel down the road from their Bangkok family home. Apparently staying overnight under the one roof with your girlfriend before marriage was a sin.

I remember first meeting Dakanda's parents early one morning over breakfast at their family home. Dakanda and I were greeted by a friendly maid who directed us to our seats.

"That's Dao, she's worked here since I was in grad school," Dakanda said.

This blew me away with amazement. No one in Australia had their own maids. The only other time I'd seen one in action was back in Africa. It felt like we were dining in at a restaurant, only far more private. The room was small and quite congested with boxes, old newspapers, manikins, exercise equipment, fancy glasses and china vases.

Dakanda and I both stood as her parents came down the stairs. Just like we practiced I clasped my hands together to resemble a prayer gesture then bowed and said, "sawadee krub". Dakanda had told me it was a sign of respect.

I remember watching Dao running back and forth with large platters of rice, making me curious about what we were eating for breakfast. "Excuse me, would you happen to have any?" Dakanda kicked me under the table before I finished my sentence. I was craving cereal, not rice.

I remember the table conversations with Dakanda's mum being free flowing and enjoyable. She was a friendly and outgoing lady who looked good for her age. She also reminded me a lot of Dakanda, howling with laughter at times when I spoke. Some of my jokes weren't intended to be jokes but no one could tell the difference. Except perhaps Dakanda's father. My interactions with him were quite different. Mr. Wattanajinda didn't speak a word the entire time which made him extremely hard to read. I've always had difficulty reading faces so being around him felt uncomfortable and I think he could sense my anxiety. Like when a dog smells fear.

I'll never forget the moment when I was left alone in the room with Mr. Wattanajinda while the girls went upstairs. I twiddled my fingers thinking of something to break the suspicious silence.

"What are the massages like here? I said.

He coughed then lit up a cigarette.

"How many of those do you take? I've never smoked before."

Again, nothing but a heavy wheeze. For a doctor he didn't appear to be in the best shape. I should've said excuse me and gone to the toilet but remember being overly determined to get a response. I then lifted up my sleeves to expose my pale arms and came out with something more creative.

"You can talk to me, I'm white" I said.

Back then I thought saying that might win him over and gain his approval to continue dating Dakanda. Isn't that what an Asian father wants to hear from a future son-in-law? I laugh and somewhat pity myself now for making such a miscalculation. Luckily my words that day didn't come back to haunt me. Dakanda's mother made a comment saying she noticed I was a bit slow but overall, the feedback was positive.

CHAPTER FORTY-TWO

I WAS RELIEVED to hear Dakanda's parents sent over more money to cover her education fees in Australia for another year. Apparently, at the same time Dakanda's father asked her whether she considered me a serious long-term partner. This made me nervous, doubting myself on staying in the relationship. I also thought Dakanda might walk away to find a man with more maturity. Our relationship, however, continued moving forward.

The following months back in Australia were overly stressful for Dakanda. Around the same time her rental lease was ending and she was having a hard time finding a new place to live.

"Why don't you move in with me?" I said.

She laughed thinking it was a joke. "You're so cute!"

Like many of my shared ideas she didn't think I was actually serious. Back then I was living by myself in my first home. I'd been fortunate enough to purchase a small apartment about fifteen minutes north of Sydney. Dad would always voice his opinion thinking the area inside was too small. "You can't even swing a cat in here!" he'd say. I'd laugh whenever he'd visit me because he'd always make unsettling cat sounds.

I remember dwelling over Dakanda's dilemma for a few days

before coming up with a creative idea. It was agreed I would move back home with my parents and she would move into my apartment. Dakanda became my tenant looking after the place and pitching in with the monthly rent. And me moving back home obeyed her parents' strict rule of living in separate houses before marriage. For me it was a no brainer. Dakanda was hesitant at first but soon warmed up to the idea once she realized living in my apartment was much cheaper than anything else on the rental market. I also offered to install a bidet for her on the toilet. I think this won her over. Bidets are everywhere in Thailand!

My parents expressed their confusion, reluctant to take me back.

"No, not again? Can't you just stay there?" Dad said.

I laughed. "I'm paying you board money," I replied.

In the few years prior I'd moved in and out of home three times so I could be walking distance from work. I lived across cheap and nasty share houses with up to ten other people. All of them were owned by wealthy Chinese ladies who weren't interested in rental agreements. Cash was their only language. I'll never forget one of them was the upper floor of a commercial building which sat above a tile shop in a poorer neighborhood of the city. Because I had trouble finding a job I enjoyed, I kept changing roles and workplaces. This frustrated my parents.

Dakanda and I timed the relocation perfectly because a few weeks later the world was struggling with the COVID-19 pandemic. Even though we were both lucky to keep our jobs, the lockdown restrictions made our relationship incredibly hard. Since we weren't allowed to meetup face to face (we did bend the rules occasionally), we relied heavily on communicating through our phones. But according to Dakanda there were days where I didn't communicate well and often days I forgot to reply back. I didn't agree with this at the time but thinking about it more she was right. And like most Asian girls, she needed regular updates throughout the day. Myself on the other hand could easily go two days without a peep. We had totally different expectations.

"I don't like texting," I said.

After that comment Dakanda gave me the silent treatment followed by a long-winded message which read:

> *I cannot be with someone that doesn't want to put an effort, doesn't want to try and adjust to me. If you say you don't like texting and that was the only option we have that time, wouldn't you take advantage of that time to put the effort and say "Okay, I'll make the most of this."*
>
> *I feel so alone and empty in this relationship. I cannot even tell you how my day was without you complaining and saying, "I don't like texting."*

It was the truth, I've never liked texting because it takes so much time and effort for me to construct a message. You can imagine how long it's taken me to write this book! Writing and responding to messages as well as calling Dakanda everyday felt outside my realm of capabilities. When I tried explaining this to her, she took it as a personal attack and thought of it as a weak excuse. Looking back now it created a distance between us, drifting Dakanda towards more of a transactional tenant than a partner.

Things went from bad to worse when she told me the horrible news. Her grandmother and one of her aunties were in hospital on ventilators, fighting off symptoms of COVID-19. At the time coronavirus was well and truly knocking people out in every country around the world. Australians had access to the Pfizer and AstraZeneca vaccines however the situation in Thailand was tougher. The only vaccine they used was the Chinese Sinovac vaccine, which was expensive, less effective and not always available. Death from the virus was also eight times more likely. Given the age of Dakanda's grandmother and her auntie's diabetes I knew their fight was going to be an uphill battle. Sadly, they both passed away within a month. I still get chills from the video, watching their bodies being carried away by people in hazmat suits.

I remember the feeling of Deja-vu when Dakanda told me. Our conversation reminded me of the day I found out about my brother. Listening to her cry over the phone I fell silent not knowing what to say. Intellectually I knew I had to say something empathetic, but aside from filler sounds like "Oh" and "aww" not much else came out. Naturally I always seem to default to asking questions.

"Is there going to be a funeral?" I said.

Dakanda brushed me off.

I've come to learn jumping in with questions is not the best thing after hearing of someone's death. People (especially girls) can be overly fragile and easily upset around the topic. It requires a high extension of empathy. Putting yourself in someone else's shoes and feeling what they're feeling. This is a very complex skill which has long been a problem for me. Growing up I remember times at funerals looking around with confusion while everyone else cringed in emotional pain reaching for tissues. Sometimes I would wipe my eyes even though they were dry. Back then I couldn't understand why I didn't respond the way everyone else was. I couldn't relate to the devastation people were feeling.

This same devastation was now in my girlfriend who was going through an enormous loss. For days Dakanda couldn't go to work, she couldn't sleep, she couldn't eat and there were even changes with her menstrual cycle. She was someone I cared for deeply and would do anything to help. But at the time I wasn't sure how to support her. I wasn't sure what to say or do to make her feel better. I couldn't relate. I'd had similar issues previously with Chaturi when one of her close family relatives passed away. I recall sending her an emoji of an apple! Whether because I didn't feel the empathy, didn't know how to express the empathy or a combination of both, I'll never know. I remember making silly jokes to cheer Dakanda up but never succeeded. It's only now I realize I didn't need to cheer her up or solve any problem, I simply needed to be emotionally present with her and grieve. But how does someone even grieve? They don't teach that in school.

After filling in COVID forms and going through the motions with the government Dakanda was granted a travel permit. She booked a one-way ticket back to Thailand, returning home to reunite with her family. Her plan was to support her parents with the mental shock, helping run errands for the wake service and organize legal paperwork around the deaths.

"Don't worry about paying anymore rent. When are you coming back?" I said.

She shrugged. At the time we both had concerns she might not be allowed back into Australia. Border security laws were changing week to week during the pandemic. I remember Dakanda needed to isolate inside a hotel for ten days after leaving the airport.

I remember a part of me was looking forward to moving back into my apartment. Mum and dad were getting under my skin. And as horrible as this sounds, part of me was relieved to have a break from Dakanda. With all the ongoing efforts to empathize and communicate the relationship was becoming increasingly hard and causing burnout for me. Family members also added pressure telling me to hurry up and pop the big question.

The last thing Dakanda said before I dropped her off at the airport was to check up on her. I thought it was best to give her a few days to settle in before reaching out. This turned out to be a serious mistake, spiraling us out of control. I received the following message after her arrival:

> I'm getting tired. You say you cannot go above and beyond. You always have excuses. I don't think I can be more patient anymore. I have told you lots of times of how the relationship can be better. I think I deserve the best relationship. The one that has intimacy,

understanding, not needing to explain myself. I need someone to do small things that matters. Before I left, I told you to check up on me. I already said it. You didn't do it. I have done my part. I cannot be waiting for you to come around on what to do. I am very tired of this relationship. Hearing stories about how my grandmother loved my parents. My grandmother was a good example of how someone is supposed to treat someone they love. At the end of the day, I think I deserve that. I don't deserve to be treat just a friend.

I remember lying in bed reading over it multiple times unsure how to respond. There was so much underlying emotion and pain in her words. I reached out to my sisters for help and we put together the following response:

Dear Dakanda
I caught up with my sister because I felt the need to get a female perspective on our situation. Wanted to express my sincere condolences for the passing of your grandmother and auntie. May they both rest in peace. My thoughts and prayers go out to you and the family over in Thailand. I really hope we can work towards solving these relationship problems together when you come back. Missing you! Lots of love.

I thought we'd nailed it. I was wrong. Dakanda replied with,

Thank you but you cannot even process things on your own. You had to ask your sisters to help you. And your message sounded like it came out of the internet. There isn't any effort to communicate more especially so that I am overseas.

I replied with a thumbs up then after that the communication fizzled. Our relationship appeared to be coming to a sad end.

CHAPTER FORTY-THREE

"I HAVE SOMETHING to tell you," Mum said.

Her serious tone gave me flashbacks of my brother's cancer. I felt relieved when her news was about my nibling. Please note nibling is the gender-neutral term for a niece or nephew.

"Sam has been diagnosed with autism and ADHD," she said.

I squinted for a moment while the information sunk in. "Is that why they cry all the time?" I replied.

Back then I was under the belief autism related only to those who are non-verbal and have special needs. I knew of ADHD because of a mischievous boy from primary school but only ever heard it in passing when talking about little boys who can't sit still in the classroom. When I first heard about the diagnosis it didn't faze me because I thought Sam was being a kid and over time they would simply grow out of it. Only now do I understand autism and ADHD go much much deeper.

Sam was a unique four-year-old who showed no interest in engagement at our family gatherings. I remember Jack and Luna wrapping Sam up in a blanket and carrying Sam through our house before unloading Sam into the toy room where they would stay for the entire time. It was the only way we could catch up with them.

Sam was non-responsive when spoken to and would run away whenever we tried approaching.

Sam also banged their head against the wall and threw tantrums (sometimes violent) whenever Jack would come home from work. Not at all from disliking their father but simply struggled with the change of having one extra body inside the house. You can imagine how difficult things must have been for Jack and Luna when they had their second child. I've watched Sam blow out their brothers' birthday candles from extreme jealousy and even heard the horror story when Sam tried to drown him in the bathtub one time. They also need to keep any sharp cutlery out of reach.

A few months passed before Luna sent everyone in our family an information brochure about the two conditions.

"What did you think?" she said.

I scratched my head. "About what?" I replied.

She laughed. "I'm going to send you an email, I think you'll find it interesting."

Apparently the first time Luna and I met each other I sat on the armrest of her chair and leaned over her while eating a sandwich. She often brings it up so my quirkiness that day made an everlasting impression.

I raised my eyebrows at the email subject title, "What is Autism?" The document gave a definition of Asperger's syndrome (high functioning autism) as a neurodivergent neurology affecting the way we communicate. It was described as a difference in thinking, influencing the way someone makes sense of the world, processing information, relating to other people and coping with situations. I resonated with some of the characteristics such as superior long-term memory and fixed interests but didn't believe I was actually on the spectrum. I had lots of friends and spoke with people every day in my job as an engineer.

Luna reminded me of the time I made mum cry when I neglected to invite her to my 30th birthday.

"She wouldn't fit in!" I said.

She smirked. "But you invited your dad."

Even though her and Jack believed I had the condition I still wasn't convinced. My parents wrinkled their nose.

"You don't have autism, you're nothing like Sam," they said.

I didn't give it much thought after that and life went on as normal. Until the day I found out my brother was taking stimulant medication for his ADHD. The news hit me like a hammer. "Holy shit!" I thought.

Astonishingly my 28-year-old brother, the successful pharmacist, homeowner and loyal father was taking prescribed medication for his behavior. Luna has shared stories of Jack being incredibly forgetful, misplacing his wallet, losing his children at the local playground, jumping into swimming pools with his mobile phone and even sometimes turning up to the wrong workplace. Both her and Jack praised how much the medication has improved his working memory.

"It's been life-changing!" Jack said.

The way he described it the medication allowed him to work more efficiently and with less effort. He could go from A to B without needing to travel via C, D and E.

I remember growing up being entertained by his silliness. I still laugh at the day Dad walked us to school while smoking a drag. Once finished, he flicked it away and kept walking ahead. Jack's eyes lit up with arousal, impulsively running after it before picking it up off the ground and taking a puff. Another time he released the handbrake while our car was parked up a steep hill. Luckily, he was smart enough to put it back on before anyone got hurt. I've already allured to the car incident at the doctors earlier. Looking back at these moments, we were just young boys having fun. Never did I see any root cause of an underlying condition for either of us causing grief. And as mentioned earlier by the time Jack reached high school most of his immaturities faded.

After hearing word of my brother's diagnosis, my parents still denied anyone in the family having these conditions. I remember mum raising one side of her mouth.

"There's nothing wrong with you!" she said.

Like many baby boomers my parents have always been conservative in their thinking and stuck in their ways. But I couldn't ignore the facts, especially when I read the conditions were inheritable. By this point I'd certainly had my fair share of hard times and desperately wanted to know why. I quickly got to work doing my own private investigation. I read and listened to these three books which I highly recommend:

"Taking charge of adult ADHD" by Professor Russell Barkley

"Look me in the eye" by John Elder Robison.

"The Complete Guide to Asperger's Syndrome" by Dr Tony Attwood.

I remember the day I self-diagnosed myself with ADHD while driving to work. I started crying after learning the condition is lifelong and often occurs alongside dyslexia. I pulled over on the freeway to gain control of my breathing and manage my emotions. When I heard about symptoms of forgetfulness and losing items, I immediately thought of all the mobile phones, cameras, cards, and keys disappearing over the years. Things I can't see with my eyes always go missing. Another symptom of ADHD is being on the go and acting as if driven by a motor which ties in perfectly with my constant need to keep busy. Impulsivity is also a primary feature which explains my quick decision making with little or no thought, and why many people over the years have laughed at my randomness and blurt out responses. The disorders emotional dysregulation and impatience, particularly when waiting in a line explains the horror of an incident one night after work.

When I was twenty-seven waiting in line for sushi a person cut in front of me to place their order. As if I was possessed by the devil, my hand seized this person's shirt, then without warning I yanked them back so hard they fell to the ground.

"Hey!" they said.

Everyone froze and took a step back, like I was about to pull out a gun. Coming to my senses I walked off with embarrassment and ordered food elsewhere. Luckily things didn't escalate further.

My stairway to the autism spectrum followed a similar route. I self-diagnosed myself in the car after listening to Tony Attwood's chapter on teasing and bullying. Tingling sensations passed through me like electricity when he spoke about kids on the spectrum retaliating and seeking revenge on others who belittle them. The penny dropped further upon hearing a strong correlation between dyslexia, ADHD and autism where it's not uncommon for someone to have all three conditions. My childhood routines of lining up and racing hot wheels cars as well as eating fruit loop cereal in a colored order seemed to correlate with the symptom of "repeated patterns of behavior". I also remember feeling a "me too" moment with many other characteristics of autism such as:

- Having a weak theory of mind. i.e. Taking longer than others to understand people's intentions, particularly when watching movies.

- Inappropriate emotional responses during conversation. i.e. sometimes I can't help but laugh at someone when they're angry or upset. This unfortunately still happens in my relationship with Dakanda.

- Remember certain things in far more detail than anyone else. i.e. Previous phone numbers, locations, dates or addresses of friends.

- Poor fine motor skills, making it difficult to hold and write with a pen and eat a sandwich which usually spills on my clothing.

- Hypersensitive to unexpected loud sounds such as motorbikes, barking dogs, hand dryers inside public toilets and the blaring of a car radio after turning the ignition.

- Hypersensitive to raw onions, certain fabrics on pillows, hair and dry sand. I cringe with discomfort at the beach when I walk along dry sand in bare feet.
- Stuttering (more so with background noise) and find it difficult selecting the right words to say when describing how I'm feeling. I loathe the question, "How do you feel?".
- Sometimes unsure of where to stand and easily lose balance when needing to dodge oncoming pedestrians in busy areas.
- Leave home wearing the wrong outfit for the occasion or get criticized for wearing mismatching colors. I often chose to wear the same clothing I've had stored in my wardrobe for many years.
- Difficultly with romantic and long-term relationships as well as mistakes choosing the right career path.

Over the years I never paid close attention to these personality traits and believed they're just part of who I am. For the same reasons some people are tall, and others are short I simply thought I was born with a very different set of skills. Never would I have picked all these symptoms were the result of an autism spectrum disorder.

Even though the answer to all my problems was staring me in the face I couldn't accept it. I needed a second opinion. Early on I chose to deny rather than believe the truth. The people around me weren't helping either.

"We love you the way you are," my parents said.

This made me paranoid and I argued within myself, second guessing whether I actually had the conditions or if I wanted an answer so bad I was prepared to believe anything. Close friends said they wouldn't be surprised if I had ADHD but expressed doubts when I mentioned the autism spectrum. I then decided to seek professional help.

CHAPTER FORTY-FOUR

MY VOICE HAD the metallic rasp of Hannibal Lector.

"I smothered his locker in my faeces," I said.

Her pen stopped writing and she gasped. "Oh!"

The psychiatrist made apprehensive filler sounds when I opened up about high school. I remember her being of European descent, sweet and innocent with timeworn features. Not the type you'd expect to be talking with crazy people.

"How do you feel about it?" she said.

My body tensed. "I don't know," I replied.

I've always had extreme difficulty answering that question and avoid it whenever possible. She continued writing while asking questions about my childhood, Jack's ADHD and my relationship with my parents.

"She thinks I'm crazy," I thought.

"It's hard to diagnose ADHD in adults," she said.

I was given homework to read a few journal articles about the disorder along with some screening questionnaires, where I rated myself on how often:

- I make careless mistakes.

- I lose my attention when doing boring work.
- I have difficulty concentrating on what people say.
- I have trouble wrapping up the final details of a project.
- I have difficulty getting things done in order when a task requires organization.
- I avoid or delay getting started on a task which requires thought.
- I misplace or have difficulty finding things at home or work.
- I'm distracted by noise or surrounding activity.
- I forget appointments or obligations.
- I fidget or squirm with my hands or feet when sitting down.
- I leave my seat in meetings or other situations when expected to remain seated.
- I have difficulty unwinding and relaxing when I have time to myself.
- I feel overly active and compelled to do things.
- I talk too much when in social situations.
- I find myself finishing people's sentences before they can finish themselves.
- I have difficulty waiting my turn.
- I interrupt others when they are busy.

When I returned with all my school reports dating back from primary school the psychiatrist smiled. "I'm going to give you something to make you feel better."

My questionnaire answers, ongoing relationship difficulties, high school experiences in addition to my brother's diagnosis was enough evidence for her to diagnose me with ADHD. Reading over my primary school reports made me angry on why it wasn't picked up earlier. Four out of the seven years teachers made comments such as, "easily distracted" and "needs to work on his listening skills." A wave of resentment consumed me as I reflected on all the situations which could have been prevented had the condition been diagnosed and managed at a younger age.

She then referred me to a clinical psychologist specializing in autism. He was a tall thin man wearing coke-bottle glasses. I really liked him because straight away I noticed he wasn't sickened by what I did in high school, but rather played it down and saw the humor in it. It felt alleviating because he understood what was going on inside my head, far better than myself. He understood the reasons behind my actions and believed I was hard done by. "Finally someone who's on my side!" I thought. When I ran through a list of all the unexplained mishaps in my life he chuckled.

"In my twenty-five years of doing this job I've never heard anyone going to hospital for forgetting to drink water," he said.

He sent me away to complete three questionnaires:

1. **Autism-Spectrum Quotient Test (AQ):**
   https://psychology-tools.com/test/autism-spectrum-quotient
   This is a diagnostic tool which measures the expression of autism-spectrum traits in an individual by one's own self assessment.

2. **The Ritvo Autism Asperger Diagnostic Scale – Revised (RAADS-R):**
   https://www.aspietests.org/raads/
   Used to identify autistic traits and as a screening instrument to assist with an autism diagnosis.

3. **Aspie-Quiz (RDOS):**
   https://rdos.net/eng/Aspie-quiz.php

Used to check for broader autism cluster (Aspie) and neurotypical traits in adults, which gives a reliable indication of autism spectrum traits prior to a diagnosis.

Unfortunately, the answer to autism is not always black and white however based on my questionnaire answers, high school experiences along with my diagnoses of ADHD and dyslexia he concluded it was highly likely I had an autism spectrum disorder. Although mild, nothing else explains the bizarre occurrences and ongoing traumas in my life.

"Your brain is wired differently to everyone else, and if I was on the spectrum, I wouldn't be worried," he said.

I smiled. The psychologist finally put me out of my misery and commended on how far I'd come since high school. I'd defied the odds because many on the spectrum inadvertently choose the wrong path by dropping out of school, hanging out with the wrong crowds and turn to alcohol and drugs.

I had the option of paying for an official assessment report which allowed me access to the government's National Disability Insurance Scheme (NDIS) but decided against it. The answer I had been longing for was staring me in the face. In my opinion any support from the government was too little too late. They need to focus their attention on the thousands worse off like my nephew.

How are you supposed to feel after finding out you've been living with disabilities your whole life? Relieved, upset, angry, remorseful, or would you rather not know? At the beginning having the answer confirmed after years of difficulty caused me some intense frustration. I remember walking into an open paddock one day, looking up at the sky and screamed. "Why the hell wasn't this picked up earlier!" Feeling the anger simmer under my skin I let off steam. My knuckles shined red from punching the wall. At the age of thirty-three I can't explain how painful it is to drift through life with a disability and not know about it. It's like kicking your legs to stop yourself from drowning when everyone else is wearing a life jacket.

It's like being taxed at 50% while the rest of the country is taxed at 30%. If typical people lived their lives carrying a bucket which needed filling, I was carrying a cup quickly filling to capacity.

I kick myself at all the wasted time and effort unnecessary tertiary education accumulating in financial debt, forgetting to lockup bikes and electric scooters only to have them stolen, leaving car interior lights turned on which result in flat batteries and all the parking fines for misunderstanding street signs.

Unfortunately, the autism spectrum, ADHD and dyslexia were unknown and misunderstood during my years of schooling. Only for severe or more obvious cases could you apply for special needs education. All those sitting in the mild category helplessly flew under the radar.

If someone needs a wheelchair, we build ramps, install elevators and provide permits, which allow these people access to priority car parking, financial benefits, reduced healthcare costs, new skills and special consideration for jobs. It's very easy to get left behind.

It took some time to reach a level of acceptance and let go of all the foolish mistakes I'd made over the past fifteen years.

ACT 3

ADULT LIFE WITH DIAGNOSIS

CHAPTER FORTY-FIVE

LEARNING THE INTRICACIES of my neurodevelopmental conditions has been paramount to moving forward. It has provided explanations into why the unexpected tends to happen. It's the reason I've needed to work hard and plan for the worst, because the worst is simply more likely to happen. Every day has been lived with an extra layer of risk.

A life full of unexpected problems takes its toll after a while. Understanding the nature of the beast is critical to mental health. I'm not surprised there's a high rate of anxiety, depression and suicide among the neurodivergent community. Although at times my anxiety can be overwhelming, I consider myself lucky to have avoided the trap of depression.

But to be honest I actually don't understand the concept of depression or suicide. It's just not logical. Why would someone want to kill themselves without knowing if their favorite rugby team might win the next NRL grand final? Who wants to miss out on enjoying their hard-earned superannuation? And wouldn't someone want to live to see the future of artificial intelligence and potentially explore mars?

Our brains control everything from our actions, thoughts,

feelings, decisions, and memories. They play an enormous role in determining who we are and act as a compass, guiding our journey through life. Imagine what might happen if something inside your brain was different, or not working the way it's supposed to.

Studies show 25 – 30% of those in prison have ADHD because of the inability to control their impulsive behaviors.[6] Associated with this is time blindness, the inability to use your foresight and see into the future, predicting things before they happen. All high school students learn these skills as they develop into adulthood however according to Dr. Russell Barkley there is a delay of about 30% when you're neurodivergent. This explains my childish behavior towards Scott and Bart when I was eighteen. Physically I was eighteen however mentally I had the maturity of a 12-year-old. i.e. 18 – 30% = 12.6 years. Had my high school misdemeanors gone unpunished, I would likely have done something much worse later on. Everything around what I did in high school links back to unmanaged symptoms of ADHD and autism.

The autistic trait of having a high sense of justice ties in with my strong desire to seek revenge and punish those who wreak havoc. Not just the Scotts and Barts of the world but also dictators like Vladimir Putin and Kim Jong Un. In my eyes they're all villains who weren't (aren't) dealt with properly.

Impulsivity and time blindness fall under the list of skills managed by our brain's executive functioning system. Located in the frontal lobe this is our brain's CEO responsible for providing us with:

- Response inhibition (The capacity to think before we act).
- Working Memory (The ability to hold information in our memory while performing tasks).
- Emotional control (The ability to manage our emotions while completing tasks).

- Sustained Attention (A capacity to maintain our attention in spite of boredom, fatigue and distractions).
- Task Initiation (The ability not to procrastinate).
- Planning and prioritization (The ability to create a roadmap to reach our goals).
- Organization (The ability to keep track of our belongings or tasks).
- Time Management (The capacity to estimate how long a task will take us and stick to a deadline).
- Goal directed persistence (The capacity to follow through with our own goals).
- Flexibility (The ability to revise our plans and adapt to change).
- Metacognition (The ability to self-monitor and self-evaluate ourselves)[5]

All of the above are weakened in the neurodivergent brain. I lost count the number of times my executive functioning has underperformed and sent me in the wrong direction. Dropping out of university to fly off to the USA with two girls in a mustang convertible is a prime example of poor planning and prioritization. Even today I still struggle in this area.

A common problem occurring alongside autism and sometimes ADHD is alexithymia. This is the difficultly to identify, understand and express one's own emotions. It makes it extremely difficult to know what you're feeling, what others are feeling and choosing the right words to describe feelings. I have no doubt this created misunderstandings and prompted feuding with people over the years, particularly in my romantic relationships, work life and overseas trip with Fatemah and Jessamine.

Alexithymia also extends into other feelings such as hunger, thirst, and needing to use the toilet. Growing up we learn what, when and how much to eat, drink and use the toilet. Through our own intuition we self-monitor and maintain ourselves which I've come to realize the hard way is not innate if you're neurodivergent.

Closely related to alexithymia is theory of mind. The ability to understand and take into account another person's intentions, emotions and reasons for their actions. I look back now and understand why I had no idea the intentions of Imani and Rohan before it was too late. And why I couldn't empathize with Luna when she told me about Jack's cancer. The neurodevelopmental delay creates a barrier between the stimulus and response, which caused me to leave the conversation and dance with my friends like nothing was wrong. But when I finally realized the full severity of his situation my brain went into meltdown, a coping mechanism used by those on the spectrum to deal with extreme feelings of overwhelm. The day I broke the broom when asked to clean the storeroom is another prime meltdown example.

At the time of writing this book my brother is in complete remission, living a happy life with his wife and two neurodivergent children. My claim to fame was driving my brother's sperm sample to the storage facility when the chemotherapy reduced his fertility. I remember buckling in the container desperate to arrive at the facility within the one hour timeframe, after which the sample dies.

"Seatbelts on!" I said to the cylindrical container, rushing through a red light. There was a one hour time limit to get it to the facility before his sample died. I remember taking on the responsibility with immense pride.

As mentioned earlier another dangerous symptom of ADHD is the need to please. In other words lacking the confidence to say no, express one's arguments, ideas and opinions. This relates back to my Africa trip where I should've been more assertive with the taxi driver, demanding him to take me to the airport. For as long as I can remember people pleasing has been engraved in my personality.

You might argue it's an admirable trait but too much of it leads to burnout.

Studies show a common link between autism and gastrointestinal problems, which I suspect has contributed to my polyps. I'd recommend any neurodivergent individual to screen their bowel and monitor their eating habits.

Autism, ADHD and dyslexia are inheritable and commonly run in families, particularly on the male side, hence most boys inherit them from their fathers. I have no doubt this is the case for me! I love my dad and will always accept him for who he is. The undying loyalty and care he shows for our family makes up for all his bad habits. In saying that many describe him as funny and different. As long as I've known him he's always had the same mullet hairdo, worn the same clothes and spoken in the same bogan accent. He's the guy you can always count on to yell, "hip hip!" during the pause in the happy birthday song. I still have vivid memories of him at his 60th birthday. We had hired a function room with a dancefloor. Towards the end of the night he walked into the middle of the dance circle, laid down on his back, elevated his legs into the air then pointed to my brother and said, "spin me!". It would be no surprise if my dad inherited these conditions from his father too. i.e. My grandfather, the one drinking and mixing beer with bricks earlier in the story. He was also quite a character. I'm sure both would have a rich collection of entertaining stories to write a book just like this!

CHAPTER FORTY-SIX

AFTER THE DUST settled around my diagnosis, I put together a list of unfinished business. I felt bad for certain people who were hurt over the course of my life as a result of my neurodivergent behaviors. I believed they needed an explanation. They deserved to know the truth on why things happened the way they did. Who knows for all I know any of them could be planning to kill me one day. It was like a belated apology or a nonreligious confession of my sins.

First up was someone I dearly missed. Dakanda Wattanajinda. We hadn't spoken for nearly 6 months. Her number was disconnected, and she'd also blocked me on social media so I wasn't even sure she'd made it safely back into Australia. There was only one way to find out.

I remember nervously returning to the hospital where we'd first met. It was hard not to stutter with the lady at reception.

"Ah, ah, excuse me, I had a procedure here last week and left my glasses behind with one of the nurses. I think her name was Dakanda," I said.

I tapped my nails on the desk while the receptionist checked her computer.

"I'm sorry, it doesn't look like she's in today, she'll be back tomorrow. Can I leave her a message?" she replied.

My cheekbones raised and I still remember the electric feel of fireworks erupting inside my body. My hands clasped onto the desk to keep me grounded because there were thoughts of jumping up to punch the air. Anything is possible when you have ADHD. The receptionist repeated her question.

"Oh yes please, tell her to call Harry," I replied.

I provided my real number but went with an alias. I knew Dakanda wouldn't pick up on Prince Harry. My plan worked like a charm. She called me from the hospital the following day.

Her soft voice gave me chills. "Hello, is this Harry?" she said.

I remember covering my mouth. After the urge to laugh went away I begged her to take me back. "How? what? you?" Dakanda sounded pleasantly surprised, pausing several times finding it hard to believe I had tracked her down. She turned me down when I asked if we could catchup, but I was persistent enough to get her new number. Within a few weeks we were back on good terms, regularly seeing each other again.

I've often thought what was it exactly which draws me to her. Why have I chosen Dakanda over anyone else? I'd had many romantic relationships fizzled over the years but there was never any urgency to rekindle with Imani, Fatemeh or Shanice etc. And whenever I'd try rekindling with Chaturi it would end in disappointment. Why did I want Dakanda back so badly?

I've come to realize it's her personality traits I find highly desirable. She has an irresistible maternal quality which I don't see much in other girls. It's that nurturing, caring and compassionate trait which makes her a brilliant choice of life partner, a perfect fit to become a mother and make for an excellent nurse.

Dakanda sits on the opposite end of the empathy and social/emotional understanding continuum. For this reason, she has continued a level of emotional support similar to that provided by my own mum when I lived at home. She compensates for many of my ADHD/autism difficulties with daily life, taking on the role of an executive secretary. Dakanda has helped me with organizational problems such as what to eat, when to buy groceries, choosing the right gifts for family and friends and what clothes to wear when leaving the house for different occasions. I remember one time she miraculously knew (before myself!) when I needed to use the toilet.

"I can hear your stomach," she said.

She has also helped with my spending habits which can sometimes lead me astray. Dakanda isn't the type to splurge on expensive female items like clothing or jewelry but rather puts her money towards more useful things such as food, transport and yoga classes. At times her friends have reached out to her for loans because they know how savvy she is.

Dakanda has been brought up with strong moral values. Integrity, honesty, generosity, thoughtfulness, reliability, and loyalty are the strongest which come to mind. Because of this I knew that once I explained my diagnoses to her and got our relationship back on track, she would be dedicated to making us succeed.

We have many differences around our physical appearance, cultural backgrounds and religious beliefs, but it doesn't bother me. Even if we had a larger age gap, because of everything I've just mentioned I would still choose Dakanda. And that's why I asked her to marry me.

But the road to marrying her was rather bumpy. Most of her family were in Thailand so she wanted a traditional Catholic wedding in the church back home. The same church of her grandmother's ashes. At first, I thought it was a lovely idea however we had a problem. In Thailand you're only allowed to marry in the Catholic church if you're actually Catholic.

"Hey dad, am I baptized?" I said.

He brushed some crumbs off his shabby Nirvana t-shirt and pondered for a moment.

"Ask your mother," he replied.

As it turned out I had some religious conversion work to do. Over the following months Dakanda and I worked on my Baptism ceremony followed by a Sacrament of Confirmation. I vividly remember kneeling in front of an archbishop, renouncing Satan while being anointed with the gift of the holy spirit. His oily thumb pressed into my forehead and drew a cross.

"Peace be with you my son," he said.

Hundreds of people inside the cathedral cheered with joy and expressed their congratulations. A tear ran down Dakanda's cheek.

"I'm so proud of you!" she said.

I smiled and thanked everyone, but deep down wasn't sure how to feel about it. It was like I'd won a gold medal at the Olympics by default. I was put on a pedestal for something I didn't quite understand or truly believe in. Hopefully I will still be allowed into heaven one day.

As our wedding day loomed, more and more Catholic-related obstacles seemed to appear. We needed to be in Thailand at least one month before the wedding date with physical proof of my baptism and confirmation certificates. I also needed to pass a canonical interview and a written exam as well as complete a confession of my sins. At one stage I started to have second thoughts.

"What happens if I don't pass?" I said.

Dakanda's eyes widened with fear. "You have to pass! We can't do it again."

"Really? But we've already paid the church," I replied.

She then shared horror stories of Thai couples postponing their weddings and losing out on their deposits after failing the requirements.

When I asked Dakanda how I can prepare or study for these Catholic requirements she shook her head. My body dropped into a valley of despair, and I became incredibly nervous. It was totally different to university where everyone studies for exams based on what they learned throughout the course. I remember thinking how can someone expect to pass if they don't know what to prepare for? Never had I heard any of this happening in Australia. Why would a Catholic church refuse to refund someone if they failed an interview or answered a question wrong in an exam? It didn't sound very holy to me.

There was also something else keeping me awake at night. Circumcision. All the men in the Wattanajinda family were circumcised and her brothers kept saying to me I was next. And when I asked Dakanda if they were joking, she'd simply laugh and not provide a clear answer.

My apprehension quickly diminished once I was sitting in front of the exam paper. I remember chuckling out loud after reading the first question.

Have you or your future partner ever been involved in the death of a previous (Ex) partner?
Please circle: YES, NO, NOT APPLICABLE

I looked around at the other Thai couples in the room for any reactions. Nothing. Dakanda smiled at me from across the table then raised a finger over her lips.

"Shhhh!" she said.

Looking back now I wonder what might've happened if I'd circled yes. Here are some of the other questions from the exam. I've written my answers at the end.

Q1 Love means:
   A. *Never giving up my ideals which my spouse should follow.*
   B. *Willingness to accept and adjust to my partner.*
   C. *Always giving in to my partner to please him/her.*
   D. *Other (specify).*

Q2 Love is best expressed in marriage by:
   A. *Continuing to say, "I love you" Remembering birthdays and wedding anniversaries.*

B. Working hard to provide for the family.
C. Fulfilling the commitment in the marriage vow.
D. Other (specify).

Q3 Love in a marriage will:
A. Have its ups and downs.
B. Be a bed of roses.
C. Be a crown of thorns.
D. Other (specify).

Q4 If the wife has a higher income, the husband should:
A. Be humble enough to accept it.
B. Be ashamed of himself.
C. Rely on the wife and take life easy.
D. Work harder and strive enough to get a higher pay.
E. Other (Specify).

Q5 On the salary, the husband should:
A. Keep a "secret account".
B. Keep a separate account.
C. Turn over everything to his wife.
D. Turn over an amount enough to cover household expenses.
E. Other (Specify).

Q6 I would allow our parents to interfere or meddle with our affairs.
A. Agree.
B. Disagree.
C. In certain situations.

Q7 I believe in physical punishment in disciplining children:
A. Agree.
B. Disagree.
C. It depends.

Q8 It is the wife's responsibility to get up at night and attend to the baby's needs:
- A. Agree.
- B. They should take turns.
- C. They should both get up.
- D. Other (Specify).

Q9 In the case of a misunderstanding between a husband and wife they should:
- A. Let it pass.
- B. Drink.
- C. Tolerate it.
- D. Give cold treatment.
- E. Out shout each other.
- F. Pray over it.
- G. Listen and talk with each other.
- H. Consult marriage counselor/priest.
- I. Go to relatives.
- J. Other (specify).

Q10 For me, sex in marriage is:
- A. Very important.
- B. Important.
- C. Not important.
- D. A duty.
- E. A right.
- F. Expression of love.
- G. Other (specify).

Q11 During sexual relations, the expectation of the husband is to:
- A. Be gentle.
- B. Take the initiative.
- C. Wait for the partners signal or cue.
- D. Other (specify).

Q12 When I notice that my partner is not in the mood for sex, I will:
  A. Get angry.
  B. Watch T.V.
  C. Go to sleep.
  D. Try to seduce him/her.
  E. Other (specify).

My answers: Q1–C, Q2-B, Q3-A, Q4-A&D, Q5-D, Q6-C, Q7-B,

Q8-D (Depends on who's working the next day).

Q9-G&J (Let it pass if too difficult).

Q10-C, Q11-C, Q12-C.

For the canonical interview Dakanda and I were handled separately by a lawyer who worked for the Catholic church. I remember swallowing hard as he entered with his polished shoes and freshly cut hair. The smell of his leathery cologne filled the room. He pulled out his notepad and quickly fired.

"Let's talk about what you were doing in high school. What was the name of your girlfriend?" he said.

I looked away telling myself not to mention anything about Scott and Bart's lockers.

"What was her name?" he repeated.

"I didn't talk to girls in high school," I replied.

"Try to remember her."

I shrugged with utter confusion. He looked me up and down with sharp eyes.

"Who was your girlfriend after high school then?" he said.

I pondered for a moment sifting through my collection of old flames. "Her name was Imani, but she never thought we were dating."

The lawyer laughed. "How often did you have sex with her?"

Before I could answer he cut me off and started asking questions about what I was studying at university. It felt more like a scorched earth campaign than an interview for marriage. Later on, he turned back asking private questions around my sex life. He wanted information around how many girls I've slept with and how many times I've slept with Dakanda.

I shook my head. "I don't keep count," I said.

Dakanda had made it clear early on in our relationship we weren't having sex until after getting married. Some of my mates joked around and said I should break up with her but unlike them staying celibate didn't bother me. There's plenty of other ways to be intimate and find pleasure.

After a few minutes of probing the lawyer finally realized I was squeaky clean. He explained he was trying to catch me out into lying about getting someone pregnant. He needed to confirm Dakanda and I were getting married for all the right reasons.

"Why didn't you just ask me?" I said.

He laughed. "It doesn't work that way,"

"Can I please ask another question?" I said.

The lawyer looked at his watch. "Quickly, my next appointment is waiting outside."

My feet fidgeted uncomfortably. "Do I need to get circumcised?"

In the Catholic church you're married for life in the name of the father and son of the holy spirit. In Thailand divorce does not exist and only in exceptional circumstances under a religious legal system can a marriage be considered for annulment. This means null and void, completely erasing the marriage from its existence. Only after signing my life away did I fully understand this!

I still remember the heavy thud when the lawyer stamped my certificate of worthiness.

We both smiled. "Congratulations Sir!" he said.

The confession was the easiest of the three, but I still needed to ask Dakanda exactly what a sin was. As you've seen illustrated in this story, I've been committing sins my whole life. Hence coming up with a list was surprisingly easy. But now I think about it, most if not all my sins were at the mercy of my undiagnosed autism and ADHD. Are they truly sins? As per definition from google a sin is a deliberate and purposeful violation of the will of God. But what about if your god is different? What if someone's actions are in fact not a violation to their god? Is it still a sin? I'll leave that for the priests and lawyers to debate.

CHAPTER FORTY-SEVEN

AT THE TIME of writing Dakanda and I have been happily married for over a year. Given we'd never lived together beforehand the first few months were a steep learning curve. Every few days I'd hear criticism around household chores like leaving dirty dishes in the sink, forgetting to clean up the kitchen bench after eating, rarely cleaning the bathroom or vacuuming the floor and refusing to take out the bins. Previous breakdowns in communication and the issues of not listening and prioritizing Dakanda also resurfaced.

At one point I even wondered whether it was all a mistake. We were in this repetitive cycle of accumulating unresolved issues causing her to reach an extreme level of frustration and unhappiness. Of course, I wouldn't realize this and do anything about it until she was yelling in my face.

"Why did you propose to me?" she'd say.

Things would calm down after I apologized but within a few weeks we'd go back to square one. It wasn't until we started seeing a relationship psychologist specializing in autism when things began to change. The psychologist had this ability to break things down in ways I could understand. During our sessions she spoke slowly, used minimal words and gave me ample time to process the intricacies of Dakanda's feelings. We both learned we definitely do love each other but are very different people speaking different love languages. Dakanda values physical touch and quality time whereas I'm heavily focused around acts of service and thus large adjustments and compromise are needed to make our marriage work.

With the help of regular ongoing sessions our marriage has survived some of the lowest times, allowing Dakanda and I to maintain a growth mindset and put the right efforts in place.

Marriages can be difficult for anyone however when you're on the spectrum they can feel impossible. As with me they can feel like there's an unclimbable mountain of work in front of you to make your partner happy. Your situation is helpless, and the only option is to run away. Not necessarily true. The reality is that with a growth mindset, you can make the relationship work once you've found the right person.

I want to make clear that being neurodivergent is not all doom and gloom. There are some highly admirable strengths and talents each of these conditions bring to the table:

Dyslexia Strengths

- Excellent visual thinkers (ability to think in three-dimensional)
- Fast and lateral problem solvers.
- Intuitive and observant when reading people.
- Articulate.
- Spatially talented.
- Creative.

Famous people with dyslexia

- Robin Williams.
- Tom Cruise.
- Winston Churchill.
- Whoopi Goldberg.

ADHD Strengths
- Endless amounts of energy, often being the life of the party.
- More open and willing to try new things.
- More likely to break away from the status quo.
- Creative and inventive.
- Driven and ambitious.
- High levels of empathy.
- Kind spirited.
- Hyper-focused on topics of interest, allowing to achieve things which seem impossible to other people.

Famous people with ADHD
- Michael Phelps.
- Albert Einstein.
- Sir Richard Branson.
- John F. Kennedy.
- Jim Carrey.
- Justin Timberlake.
- Emma Watson.
- Ryan Gosling.
- Woody Harrelson.

Autism Strengths
- Absolute loyalty and reliability in friendships.
- Ability to pursue personal theory despite conflict.
- Listening without judgement.
- Technical and mathematically gifted.
- Possess a high sense of social justice and integrity.
- Original and unique in problem solving.
- Likely to thrive on routine and clear expectations.
- Very honest.
- Determined and persistent.
- An expert on specific topics.

- Aware of sounds that others cannot hear.
- Attention to details and errors that others do not see.
- Exceptional at remembering things that others have forgotten.
- Humorous in a unique way.
- Higher chance of attending university after high school.

Famous people with autism

- Elon Musk.
- Bill Gates.
- Dan Aykroyd.
- Anthony Hopkins.
- Sir Isaac Newton.
- Daryl Hannah.
- Susan Boyle.

Some of the most successful people in the history of the world have lived and survived with neurodevelopmental conditions. Without them we'd have a poor understanding of space, time and gravity, we wouldn't be using Microsoft on computers, our movies and artwork would be dull and there'd be no future trips planned to explore Mars.

The world needs more of us. Today with the health risks of the COVID-19 pandemic, climate change, cyberattacks and nuclear warfare our world is facing many serious challenges. And I don't believe we can overcome them without neurodiversity. We are the secret ingredient to longevity for our planet. The world is also ready to accept our different kinds of minds. More and more people are starting to understand our enormous strengths and the value add we bring to society. The future is bright!

At the time of writing diagnosis rates for autism and ADHD are on the rise in Australia, with children receiving the help they need much earlier in their lives. No longer do we think of autism as a rare condition in childhood. Older generations who weren't diagnosed as kids are now parents of autistic children and have reshaped how we talk about it and what is means to be autistic.

Autism is on the Australian National Disability Insurance Scheme (NDIS) and at the time of writing is driving a complex debate for the federal government. A major budget pressure being considered is how funding should be delivered to support Australians with autism. 35% of all participants on the NDIS report autism as their primary disability.[1]

Jack and Luna receive financial assistance to cover professional services for both Sam and their son who also has autism and ADHD. Without this help they would certainly struggle to get by. I remember before joining the NDIS Luna considered selling her car to cover the cost of Sam's ongoing psychology and speech pathology appointments.

Although Sam can be a very challenging child at times, I want to stress they are incredibly talented when it comes to Lego. At the age of five Sam finished building a Technic model of a Ferrari which was categorized difficult for 16-year-olds. Sam is also highly intelligent and not afraid to use big words and speak their mind.

"What was the trajectory of the North Korean missile?" Sam asked me one time.

I scratched my head and thought to myself it was actually a good question and also wanted to know the answer.

I've learnt so much from watching Sam grow up and interestingly relate to some of their behaviors. Luna has also mentioned similarities between the way we both communicate.

At the time of writing Sam is currently ten years old and identifies as non-binary (neither male or female). This is the reason I have used different pronouns. Sam has also attended school wearing a dress and even been courageous enough to stand up and explain to the class the reasons why. Going back in time if I'd rocked up at Egan High one day wearing a dress, I'm certain Scott, Bart and many others wouldn't let me live another day.

Australia now has its first minister for autism to help craft its first national autism strategy. The federal government are planning to boost understanding among key professions and the wider community, make education and employment more accessible as well as provide better support for families. We can also expect more autistic faces in Australian sport and media, while public spaces and transport will cater to the sensory differences for the neurodivergent community. South Australia already has the ball rolling persuading universities to introduce new modules in their teaching degrees around autism, disability and inclusion. They're also working on getting an autism inclusion teacher into every public primary school.[1]

With more and more teenagers getting diagnosed the department of education has mandated high school teachers write education plans to support their students individual learning if they are experiencing difficulties.

I spoke with a friend of mine recently who is an English teacher.

"We are very well briefed, more than ever high schools are across the individual learning needs of students," she said.

Unlike my time at Egan High, the curriculum now in Australia has changed so that content and achievement standards allow continuous learning for all students with disabilities and additional learning needs. Teachers now have the flexibility to tailor and adjust their instructions and assessment strategies in ways for neurodivergent students to demonstrate knowledge, skills and understanding equal to that of their peers. The curriculum caters for gifted and talented neurodivergent students too!

Governments are also encouraging corporate companies to build their knowledge and provide educational workshops for thousands of employees on the importance of diversity, inclusion and belonging. They are starting to consider their working environments such as bright lights, loud noises and kitchen smells to reduce sensory overload. The time is certainly now to seek a diagnosis and get the support you need.

Arguably the biggest superpower which develops naturally within someone neurodivergent is resilience 2.0. Similar to rubber which returns to its original shape after applying a force, the same also applies to the neurodivergent brain. Because the person is thrown into greater amounts of stress and pressure from the daily grinds of life and high school, they not only return to their original self but become more fit, capable and strong. As a result they become better in performing under pressure, dealing with and solving a crisis compared to other neurotypicals.

Without knowing I've used this superpower in combination with many other strategies to stay on the right path and achieve success. If I can do it, you can too!

CHAPTER FORTY-EIGHT

IN ADDITION TO married life with Dakanda and our sessions with the psychologist I must mention another influential factor helping me to live my best life. Medication.

Like it or not stimulant medication is the most effective way of treating symptoms of ADHD. This is backed by years of research. For myself, Jack, Sam and thousands of others prescription drugs have lowered the obstacles getting in the way of creating new habits and applying strategies to fill in neurodivergent gaps. There is nothing wrong with taking medication and anyone with ADHD should at least give it a go. I have no shame in saying a 15mg dose of Ritalin in the morning and another 10mg in the afternoon improves my executive functioning and allows me to perform at my best. At the beginning I battled with side effects of dizziness and loss of appetite but after a while your body adjusts and the benefits seep in. Jack has noticed large improvements in his efficiency with household chores like laundry, washing dishes and changing linen.

If we dive into the neurobiology, ADHD causes an imbalance of chemical uptake in the brain. Dopamine and norepinephrine are important chemicals (or neurotransmitters) which enable the brain to transmit signals, allowing us to function in our everyday lives. In the ADHD brain these are heavily absorbed at the back and very little at the front (prefrontal cortex). Medication works like placing a sock over a vacuum cleaner, blocking the uptake of these chemicals at the back and thus allowing more absorption to take place at the front. A person on medication can utilize the full potential of their prefrontal cortex. Who wouldn't want that?

I think of ADHD in the same way as diabetes. Diabetes is an imbalance of insulin which we treat with prescription drugs to normalize levels in the bloodstream. It's the same for ADHD except instead of insulin we are normalizing the brains neurotransmitters dopamine and norepinephrine. I also relate to ADHD medication like most people relate to coffee. People drink coffee in the morning to kick-start their day whereas I take a customized caffeine pill which kick-starts my day in different ways.

To help manage my ADHD I live by eight key rules recommended by Dr Russell Barkley, a professor who has published more than 300 scientific articles on ADHD. The following are printed and stuck on my bedroom wall:

1. Stop the action! Buy yourself time before you respond.

2. See the past and then the future. Use your mind's eye to see what's coming.

3. Say the past and then the future. Use your minds voice to say what you intend to do before doing it.

4. Externalize key information. Rely on something besides your memory like a notepad and pen.

5. Feel the future. Stay motivated by having a physical picture or message printed out on the wall.

6. Break it down and make it matter. Splitting large tasks into small chunks with small rewards can bring the future a lot closer.

7. Make problems external, physical and manual to simplify problem solving. For example, write it down or lay out on a table.

8. Have a sense of humor. Accept your imperfections and get on with life!

Given autism is linked to the brains wiring, medication is not effective at treating all the symptoms. Based on my experience ADHD medication still has knock-on positive effects. It allows me more time to consider my actions and responses, especially when having conversations. It minimizes stuttering and autism-related social blunders such as saying the wrong thing.

The full extent on how the autistic brain is wired differently is still not fully understood. Overall, we're all wired differently however the general consensus is that autism usually involves overconnectivity within brain regions and underconnectivity between brain regions. I'll avoid going any deeper than this for now.

Also hanging up in my bedroom is a self-affirmation reminder taken from Professor Tony Attwood's book on autism spectrum disorder. Tony is considered one of the world's foremost experts on the condition.

I am not defective, I am different.

I will not sacrifice my self-worth for peer acceptance.

I am a good and interesting person.

I will take pride in myself.

I am capable of getting along with society.

I will ask for help when I need it.

I am a person who is worthy of others respect and acceptance.

I will find a career interest that is well suited to my abilities and interests.

I will be patient with those who need time to understand me.

I am never going to give up on myself.
I will accept myself for who I am.

I regularly read out loud what's on my bedroom wall because I not only see it, but also hear it which drills in the growth mindset necessary to keep going.

I also recommend investing in regular exercise and meditation. You don't necessarily need to get involved with a sporting club but just a walk/run through a park at least three times a week will calm the mind and relieve some anxiety from the chaos of life. I would not be where I am today without the joys of competitive running and breakdancing with likeminded friends around the city.

To meditate simply find a quiet spot, pull out your phone and set the timer for 10 – 15 minutes. Once comfortable close your eyes and count your breathing. I also focus on something which has nothing to do with past trauma or anything making me sad, such as my hands resting on my knees or my feet in contact with the ground.

To battle problems with hydration I now use a smart drink bottle called a HidrateSpark. It's an electronic bottle which connects to an app on my phone via Bluetooth. The app measures my daily water intake and lights up, reminding me when it's time to drink. It's amazing, I haven't been hospitalized since!

Since autism primarily affects the social parts of our brain, communication and social skills has been the greatest of challenges. I could write another entire book on this topic but one critical piece of information which helped me was the 55/38/7 formula. i.e. communication is broken up into the following three elements:

- 55% Non-verbal (body language and facial expressions).
- 38% Tonality (voice).
- 7% Verbal (the words we speak).[9]

I'd spent my whole life focusing and worrying about the words coming from my mouth. According to the above formula this only makes a tiny impact on the outcome of the message being communicated. In other words, I'd been wasting my time. It wasn't until I worked on improving my body language, facial expressions and tone of voice when I saw results.

There are many places on the internet to help in these areas however I recommend Vanessa Van Edwards, who is a behavioral investigator at a research lab in the USA. She's published two books which share all the codes and hacks to read people's emotions and help navigate yourself in social situations. These are:

- Captivate: The science of succeeding with people.
- Cues: The secret language of charismatic communication.

Her website also provides loads of other useful information on social skills. Check out www.scienceofpeople.com.

CHAPTER FORTY-NINE

OUR BRAINS ARE malleable which means anyone (neurodivergent or not) can learn new skills and work on areas of improvement. It's not about changing your entire personality but using self-awareness learned from the knowledge of autism, ADHD and dyslexia to manage yourself better. I am still growing, still learning and vigilant about old temptations and patterns of behavior which could get me in trouble again. Initially I felt ashamed having to go through a life full of problems but getting diagnosed, understanding why then implementing the right strategies along with writing this book has facilitated the healing process and provided a level of closure. I no longer judge myself for past actions but celebrate the person I am today. It's also never too late to apologize and I'm grateful for the opportunity people have given me to explain the reasons behind my silly behavior.

Given the superpower strengths and robust resilience of autism, ADHD and dyslexia, I consider myself lucky to be born neurodivergent. As Professor Tony Attwood puts it,

We're bright threads in the rich tapestry of life with a different way of perceiving, thinking, learning, and relating. We have a strong desire to seek knowledge, justice, truth and perfection with a different set of priorities than one would expect. We prefer to solve a problem than satisfy the social/emotional needs of others. We value creativity over co-operation and are renowned for speaking our minds, being honest and having a distinct sense of humor.

There's certainly nothing wrong with any of that. Life is a rollercoaster for everyone. I hope the strategies I've mentioned work for you as they have for me. At the time of writing, I am still married to a beautiful Thai lady, a proud homeowner, drive around in a new Toyota Rav4 Hybrid and hold a secure job for a global medical technology company. I don't plan to stop growing anytime soon and neither should you! Show the world what your neurodivergent brain is capable of and leave a legacy people will remember forever.

CHAPTER FIFTY

"IS THERE ANOTHER table?" I said.

The waiter pointed to a booth around the corner. "Perfect!" I thought. We needed more privacy.

Scott Read was second after Dakanda on my reconciliation list. I had tracked down his phone number from the yearbook then messaged him out of the blue to arrange a meeting. Because of the COVID-19 lockdowns we needed to postpone several times, but I was persistent to make it happen. Ever since my self-discovery, I felt the need to explain myself, apologize and shout him out to a nice dinner. Even though it had been a long time I still felt bad after the way things ended.

Nervously straightening my collar, the phone vibrated.

"I'm running late," Scott said.

I replied cautiously, "Let me know when you're here." I remember reading over my welcome greeting and notes. It felt more like a job interview to me than a catchup.

Launching from the table I powerwalked to the restaurant entrance then dried my sweaty palms behind my knees. I noticed his lean figure in the line. He wore a t-shirt, shorts and thongs which surprised me given the effort I'd gone to dressing up. Scott's red hair had faded to a light brown, but his face still looked the same. Smiling with an open posture I offered a handshake.

"Hey long time!" I said.

He looked down at me then panned across the room with a puzzled face.

"This is a bit weird mate," he replied.

Nothing at all about our catchup felt weird to me. As I've done many times before when masking, I still nodded in agreeance. As we sat down Scott mentioned his suspicion when I first reached out to him.

"I thought this was a setup, I didn't believe you were for real," he said.

I acted surprised. "Oh, not at all, I just wanted to apologize for what happened in high school,"

Scott shook his head. "There's no need to apologize mate,"

He then pointed to his chest, and I noticed the tattoo of the Australian southern cross on his forearm.

"I can see you got heart." Scott said.

His words that night confirmed he hadn't held any grudges from high school. Unlike myself Scott's voice and breathing pattern was slow and well controlled. I was talking to a very different boy from the one I knew fifteen years ago.

"I need to explain why I did it," I said.

After sharing my diagnoses and linking it back to what happened he responded with a question which threw me off my chair.

"What did you do again? All I remember is some missing shoes," he said.

I leaned forward over the table with a crinkled nose. "You don't remember the tablet incident?" I remember thinking to myself, "How can he possibly have forgotten?" My main objective for our meeting was to clear the air, but there was no air to clear. And the only thing polluting it was me!

He laughed when I told him the effort I went to with the security cameras to break into his locker.

"Jeez, you must have really not liked me," he said.

I was also shocked with his cloudy memory of the verbal abuse. He remembered being a loudmouth but couldn't pinpoint anything specific he'd done to upset me.

"You've been thinking about this for a while, haven't you?" Scott said.

I nodded as he continued. "I can see it's affected you a lot more than me. The way I see it, we were just kids doing silly things to each other."

I came to realize he'd moved on a long time ago. What happened between us in high school meant nothing to him. While I'd been holding onto things this whole time, Scott had grown up and matured into an adult. We enjoyed each other's company at the restaurant for over an hour, asking about our families and what everyone was up to. It was like nothing bad had ever happened between us. Scott had left the past behind and was now married with two children.

Our two different perspectives here illustrate the internal forces of autism. When you're on the spectrum it's much harder to let things go and forget past trauma. It explains my ongoing fear of dogs decades after being bitten when I was twelve. It also explains why my dad is petrified of getting into an elevator after having a bad experience when he was younger. When you're on the spectrum you also have a very different set of priorities than would be expected of other people. In other words, what's important to you is not important to most others.

Leaving the restaurant, I drove back home with a transformed view of Scott Read. He was no longer the verbally abusive high school bully. He was now an old friend who today has my respect. Scott has even supported the writing of this book. I often wonder if I ever reached out to Bart whether I'd have the same success? My mates tell me not to bother.

ACKNOWLEGEMENTS

WRITING A BOOK is harder than I thought and even harder when you're neurodivergent. It's a marathon, not a sprint but certainly more rewarding than I could ever have imagined. None of this would have been possible without my beautiful wife Dakanda supporting me every step of the way. She has stood by me during every struggle and all my successes. A true partner for life.

I'm extremely grateful for the professional feedback and advice from my editor Liz Monument. She has been a brilliant coach steering me towards fine tuning my first draft into a finished item and suggesting avenues for publication. Shout out to Theodore Belcastro for the referral and ongoing words of inspiration.

Writing a book about the story of your life is a surreal process. A very special thanks to Luna and Jack for being open and transparent around Sam's autism/ADHD diagnosis and planting the seed for the creation of this book and bringing my stories to life.

To my family. My parents for their support during those dark and desperate years as well as funding my treatments at the dyslexia therapy centre. To my siblings and cousin thank you for your encouragement.

Finally, to all those who have played a part of my getting there:

Jacob Egan, Alex Koumoundouros, Andrew McKay, Nick Dunn, Leigh Mullenger, Jackson Ha, April Supapong, Jerry Jenkins, Vanessa Van Edwards, Dr Tony Attwood, Dr Russell Barklay, Clayton Hobbs and all the team at Author Services Australia.

ABOUT THE AUTHOR

TRAVIS ALEXANDER IS a science and engineering master's graduate working in the medical technology industry.

Growing up, he was faced with many unexplained hiccups, delaying his development into adulthood.

Through self-discovery and coming to terms with his autism, ADHD and dyslexia diagnoses, Travis is now a passionate advocate for the neurodivergent population. He aims to inspire others to live their best lives.

When he's not telling stories, Travis enjoys breakdancing, running and spending quality time with his wife.

For more information about Travis, visit his website at:

www.travisalexander.com.au.

REFERENCES

1. Chrysanthos, N. (2024). Thousand-fold increase: What is driving the rise of autism? *Sydney Morning Herald*. https://www.smh.com.au/politics/federal/thousand-fold-increase-what-is-driving-the-rise-of-autism-20240221-p5f6sa.html

2. Chrysanthos, N. (2024). Beautiful minds: Inside the identity politics of autism. *Sydney Morning Herald*. https://www.smh.com.au/politics/federal/beautiful-minds-inside-the-identity-politics-of-autism-20240221-p5f6sc.html

3. Chrysanthos, N. (2024) The steps being taken to get better treatment for Australia's autistic people. *Sydney Morning Herald*. https://www.smh.com.au/politics/federal/the-steps-being-taken-to-get-better-treatment-for-australia-s-autistic-people-20240221-p5f6se.html

4. Aspect (Autism Spectrum Australia) website (2024) https://www.aspect.org.au/about-autism

5. Dawson, P. & Guare, R. (2023) *Smart but Scattered*. https://www.smartbutscatteredkids.com/

6. Dr Dianne Grocott, *ADHD Multimodal Therapies* (2022)

7. Barkley, R.A & Benton, C.M (2022) *Taking charge of Adult ADHD*, 2nd edition.

8. Attwood, T *The Complete Guide to Asperger's Syndrome*. (2008)

9. Edwards, V.V *Captivate – The Science of Succeeding with People*. (2018)

10. Bowel Cancer Australia website https://www.bowelcanceraustralia.org/bowel-cancer/bowel-cancer-facts/

www.ingramcontent.com/pod-product-compliance
Lightning Source LLC
Chambersburg PA
CBHW020522080526
44583CB00013B/693